DOORS OF ETERNITY

DOORS OF ETERNITY

by

Sibyl Harton

MOREHOUSE-BARLOW CO.
NEW YORK

Copyright © 1965 by Sibyl Harton

FIRST AMERICAN EDITION
March, 1965

Printed in the United States of America
by Haddon Craftsmen, Inc.

To

REX

Brother and Friend

ACKNOWLEDGEMENTS

I should like to thank Burns & Oates for their kind permission to quote from mediaeval poems adapted by Nevile Watts and published in *Love Songs of Sion*, Punch Publications for their permission to quote a verse by Virginia Graham first printed in *Punch* on the 8th August, 1945, and A. P. Watt & Son for their permission to quote from Sir Henry Newbolt's poem *March 5, 1921* published by John Murray Ltd. in *A Perpetual Memory and Other Poems* by Sir Henry Newbolt.

CONTENTS

	page
Preface	11
Glory	13
Suffering	31
Sacrifice	52
Detachment	74
Redemption	96
Separation	119
Death	134
Glory	155

PREFACE

I recall as if it were but yesterday that day when I knew that I should write about death. Doubtless it was no sudden idea; it would follow in natural sequence my book *On Growing Old*. At Evensong in the Cathedral that Sunday afternoon there was some especially noble music played, or sung, with great sensitivity (how often I have wished I could remember what it was), which had stirred my depths; and suddenly I was alight with the thought of death. I came home to the Deanery tea-table emotionally exalted by the music and the creative stirrings which it had roused. Unable to contain the excitement, I announced impetuously that I was going to write about death, death lovely and precious, serene and holy, not diminishing but perfecting, death welcome. I was in love with death. Nanita was there (she still remembers) and Peter, and they seemed rather surprised and uncertain what to say.

I little knew how soon death was to invade the home and put an end to our tea-table, bringing me experience and knowledge beyond anything I could imagine, beyond resistance, beyond doubt. Quickly there came a letter from a priest, begging me to write at once, write while grief was upon me, for the sake of the many people who need help and comfort in bereavement. But that was impossible. The meanings and validity of an experience cannot be known and judged upon its first assault, it needs to be absorbed into the fibres of one's being, to be lived with and endured through time, to be 'recollected in tranquillity', before it can be raised above the narrowly personal and reveal its universal value and relation. It has to be weighed and measured in relation to one's weaknesses as well as one's strengths, and for this, time is the vital ally. So the years have passed whilst death has been received and lived with in an ever-enlarging and enriching context, until at last the book can be written. To write of death requires poetry. Where, please, is the holy poet?

To whom are due my thanks? The text will supply obvious answers, but who can recognise all the sources and influences where much is owed or little? Wherever the way lies, between hedgerow or on highway, under any sort of sky, alone or in a crowd, the insights and showings come: usually when one least expects them. One cannot measure the power which is shed abroad by the generous prayer of contemplative nuns or by the sudden interest and sympathy given by a stranger: there is no need to, but grateful acknowledgement and love is carried in the heart, and conviction grows that in no creative design does one stand alone. "As for myself, I am giving thanks to Providence," wrote l'Abbé Breuil after his first major prehistoric discovery. Nothing further need be said, except that the Supreme Design never obscures its parts.

SIBYL HARTON

GLORY

Heaven and earth are full of thy glory. This is the assertion and what are we to make of it? Not a matter for doubt or for argument, it stands as a proclamation: a great gate standing wide open, inviting entry. The whole earth is full of His glory. Does a knowledge of God begin with a sight of the glory or is glory the reward of knowing Him? Who first saw God as glory? And how was the concept of glory reached? These are fascinating questions to explore.

'Glorious' is said of things, people, places, episodes, experienced as easily and commonly as a child eats the food it enjoys. Perhaps it is with more caution that we use the word 'glory', but we know its significance. We recognise it effortlessly though variously, according to the sort of people we are, as a splendour, an honour, greatness, perfection, as a revelation of some superlative worth. Used in a song, a poem, a speech, glory declares its accepted meaning; assuming, that is, that you can hear, that you can read. Thousands of years ago the Hebrew poet cried that the heavens declare the glory of God. Do they do so to-day, or was that statement only of temporary value? Are they indeed the same heavens?

A boy born and reared in an old decaying back street of a great industrial city, receiving his schooling there, going for his holidays to relatives in similar places, may be so clever that he studies his way through school, through university, to a science doctorate: yet he is unaware of the sublime picture of the night sky, he cannot receive its declaration, for he is unable to see it when circumstances at last provide the opportunity. The calm brightness of the Milky Way, the spectacular brilliance of the hanging planet, these are not for him. He may, when invited, lift his glance to the silent sailing moon, he may look, but there is no accompanying opening of the interior eyes which will enable him to take hold of, to apprehend in even a small degree, that upon which he looks. He that has eyes, has ears, let him see, let him hear, for the life of the eye and the ear is within. It is more likely that for such a person the heavens will be found in some artefact of modern man, in the keen impassive beauty of a great machine, of the newest airport, or in a great steel factory, where function, precision, skill, dedication to a useful purpose, all combine to touch the mind and spring open the ego to a perception of greatness and grandeur beyond and above itself. So, there is an acknowledgement of glory, although God if unknown must be unacknowledged. For anything anywhere at any time may suddenly become a channel of light, unexpected and rare, in which we see for the first time and with a new understanding, some value hitherto unperceived, some quality which we have supposed might exist but which now becomes a certainty: I see, I know. But there are many different levels in the reality exposed, many degrees in the depth of revelations, even as one star differs from another in magnitude. The showing that comes to us may illuminate our knowledge of the natural world, its hidden qualities and powers, it may enlighten the mind with regard to truth in any sphere we are searching, or it may uncover treasures of heavenly realities which outdistance dialectics. Any form of art, painting, sculpture, music, words, even pursuits which are but mildly creative, such as fishing and bird-watching, mountaineering and sailing, can take you into a spacious place beyond yourself. And beyond the sensations, the impressions and the images, beyond the weaving of thought, there is an exaltation of spirit which is essentially related to glory. All great art should perform, in varying degrees, the priestly function of mediating to men the truth, the majesty, the triumph of pure being and of exalting men into more than normal communion with essential Being, which is God. In this experience is a well-spring of joy, perhaps also a pain of unutterable longing; all the deepest emotions are played upon, deep in proportion to the nature of the recipient, and from the stirring may come love, adoration, noble resolves or a creative surge. Glory is abroad.

Do we ponder our way from the objects of the physical world which surrounds us, from scientific certainties, from accepted intellectual satisfactions and enlightenments, towards the mystery of glory, or is it that the prevenient mystery lights up, makes real, gives meaning, to all of our many levels of existence and perception in the organic and natural world in which we live? The watcher in the woods, the scientist in his laboratory, the philosopher brought to prayer, all may be caught in the glories which enlarge and inflame us, but their recognition demands response from different depths in man's being. We need our outward senses and our intellects to be aware of and to receive the glory in creation and in the works and deeds of men, but we require the soul's interior faculties to perceive what is beyond the light of natural knowledge. For there is a ladder of communication and in the hierarchy of creation the displayed glories enlarge and deepen in the ascent. The more directly the acknowledged presence of Deity manifests His glory, the more interior and elevated must be the soul's powers of reception; the greater the soul's awareness of such pure glory of spirit, the more it knows that the fullness of its reality must infinitely transcend any glimpses given in this terrestrial life. Yet what the eye of the spirit is even here empowered to see is sufficient promise of the unimaginable rapture and bliss which shall be given to us when we come into eternity, into that place which is God. For it is exactly there, into eternity, into infinitude, to perfection, to that than which no greater can be conceived, that the thought of glory leads us.

To whom comes a showing of glory, a recognition of it, a conviction of its certainty? What mental powers does it demand, what emotional development? What preparation, if any? Do animals know glory? This we cannot say, for although our life is lived alongside theirs, seeing hearing touching them daily, there is actually so slight a communication that we cannot penetrate the mystery of their existence, though we readily (and sentimentally) give it some attributes of our own. How strange it is that there is this immensity of creaturely life surrounding us with almost no communication, and yet an appreciable amount of dependence. It is certain that creatures have awarenesses of a reality beyond their natural sense-life, and from our observation of these we may make deductions upon which our imagination builds; but the building is with materials which have no factual validity except in the builder's own country, and in that country the only certain realities are beauty, emotional power, symbolic value, displayed to us in art and literature. Once having read it you would never forget, for instance, Kenneth Grahame's deeply moving description, in *The Wind in the Willows*, of Rat and Mole hearing at the time of the dawn, music beautiful, new, strange, which transports them beyond their normal world, possessing them utterly and compelling them to follow it to a place where they are given a sight of Him, Friend and Helper, to whom in awe and love they instinctively give worship. This powerful imagination may be valid, animals may have a capacity to receive glory, to be touched by it, to respond: many of us may have seen some indications of such an interior faculty in a horse, a cat, a dog: but we can speak only in terms of possibility, and we are not far from the realms of faerie. It is not unimportant that this showing of glory came to the two small animals of the wild when they were engaged on an unselfish and strenuous errand of mercy, searching for a neighbour's lost child.

Has a child the power to know that which is adorably other than and beyond itself and its sensible surroundings? How early does it acknowledge something more than contentment conveyed through its senses? Of course children vary in capacities: one will have a nature predisposing it to quietness, to solitariness, to thoughtfulness, which another appears to lack: but, in general? It is the testimony of a succession of poets that in their earliest years they recognised a glory on the earth which clothed all common things in a celestial light. From infancy they know "the glory of bright shoots of everlastingness"; they accept the shapes of normal things in their surroundings as splendid, pure, rich, as treasures displayed by God, so that this world really resembles His eternity of perfection: and they love everything. Yet poets speak for all of us, having as their unique cradle-gift the power to see in light and declare as plain that which we fumble and guess at in darkness. Are the childhood experiences of Traherne, Vaughan, Wordsworth, de la Mare, ours also? Could they uncover buried recesses, many ordinary and humble people might recall youthful occasions when some very ordinary object suddenly became transparent and the wonder of its essential self was revealed. The thing became different and appeared more truly itself, yet when the child related its wonderful discovery, in such language as it had, the adults failed to show any genuine enthusiasm. They answered with no understanding sympathy, and the child felt repulsed. Perhaps it is because the normal child is without the words required to fix these apprehensions of glory in the memory that they fade away, fall into an oblivion; later we forget how to remember that once we saw and knew how God Himself encloses us in all the things of the world, therefore bestowing on us continual felicity. But that this is indeed the infant's birthright may explain the largesse of that heavenly smile which the babe in its first months bestows so bountifully upon the world.

Who should know more of glory than lovers? That is why "it is better to have loved and lost than never to have loved at all". Sauntering along the street busy with Saturday morning shoppers, his glance is caught and held by a girl standing immobile in front of the fishmonger's great marble counter spread elegantly with the smooth shining sea-food. Is she simply pondering her choice, deciding what her short purse can best afford, or is she in a reverie remote from fish, this ordinary young woman of the city? No matter, for in that instant he has seen not an ordinary girl but a perfection. Love is born, glory intervenes: who can say which is first? Again, the others see merely that she is looking down at the kitten playing on the floor but he, already possessed by love, sees in her face an expression revealing a galaxy of virtues, tenderness, amusement, pity, and to him the slant of the bent head continuing the line of her supple neck is a sudden smiting of glory: and it hurts. "Stand still," she cries, for in his upstretched arm, swinging the brush to and fro in vigorous strokes as he works hard to finish painting the fence, she catches a sudden sight of the nobility and beauty in movement of which hitherto she has been all unaware, and her adoration would see him like that for ever.

GLORY

Love laces a lightning of pain through her heart. But no vision stays, and this fades; and none of the passers-by had seen more than Tom's rather clumsy efforts in an unaccustomed job. The mother in an ecstasy of thankfulness bows over her last-born child, caught in a wonder at the glory of new life, in a passion of love for what actually had been unwanted. Friend looks at friend, and often having found him slightly distasteful, irritating, trivial, one day sees suddenly in a flash the sheer beauty of his soul as soul, and thereafter never quite loses the power of seeing him again in that reality, or at least can recall the knowledge given: even as a torch flashed up into the dark corner of a well-known passage lights up for the first time some unsuspected perfection of mediaeval moulding in the frieze and thus, as food for the memory, permanently enriches knowledge of that place.

Yet recalling in memory is far from being the same thing as the original experience which, alas, loses force, fades away, may indeed become wholly forgotten. The strongest love, being finite and human, can falter, be untrue and die, that which is momentary and fragile may subsequently be denied, that which was accepted effortlessly has later to be learnt with labour and a price for it paid. All of which adds up to the fact that the vision of glory comes, goes, and cannot be prophesied or commanded. And there are so many degrees in the givenness of the vision splendid. The world is indeed full of glory, but we receive it, we take hold of it, in different ways, by many different means. A music-lover is exalted by the perfection of composition and of playing to which he is listening. His trained hearing and his expectant emotions are gathered to a point of concentration on the art, to which he responds with facility, with knowledge, with delight, moved to tears, to laughter, to reverence, as it impels. He admits the brilliancy, the beauty, the perfection: but that is because he elects to listen, having cultivated his tastes and his personal capacities for this very thing — for satisfaction through the apprehension of glory in music. Yet his deep contentment, flowing through the fibres of his being and bringing true exaltation of soul, is in a different category of experience from that sudden inrush of awareness which takes no account of any man's will, desires or preparation, but assaults him irresistibly in the depths of his being. There can be a revelation of glory which opens a man's heart independently of his expectation or volition, an opening which will close so quickly, perhaps never again to be uncovered on the same scene, although perhaps never to be forgotten. Surely there cannot be a man who has not known the moment when he is staggered out of time into the silence beyond? Forget it he may, but his deep centre holds the experience. And the view of that other country may be granted anywhere, not necessarily in the stillness and lonely beauty of landscape or seascape, but in the city of crowded humanity, where the wind, rain and shafts of sunlight may be the most that is normally seen of nature. Day after day the journey to work is made in the bus whose cramped and uneasy conditions never vary; yet on one morning and one morning only, with no warning premonitions, she suddenly sees her fellow-travellers in a light of love, sees them in this display to be truly lovable. Her soul flows out to them all in a wave of goodwill and of joy because of their goodness: everything is new, is born afresh. The exaltation passes before she reaches her stop, but not the certainty of the experience nor the truth which remains in the intellect, that love rules, that love alone maintains the equilibrium of all creation.

When and wherever comes this eruption of glory it will be unexpected, sudden as a single roll of thunder on a cold day. For years he has looked at buildings, for architecture is his passion, his hobby, and his knowledge of it is sound, rich and lively. Why is it, then, that only on one particular day when he is gazing at a much-loved mediaeval façade, are his senses suddenly seized and torn open to permit an uprush of insight into a unity which underlies and transcends all forms of beauty, binding all the arts into a supersensory reality, all thought into unity of being? He is giddy with great revelation: but time stands still for only a moment; he recovers, and sky, place, passing people, become again what they ordinarily seem. He may never again win the vision but he keeps the memory, for in that timeless moment he was granted the freedom of that other kingdom, and he can say to his soul, "I am part of it and it of me." We do not know the times and seasons of this kingdom, so we can never account for the presentation of the unexpected insights and revelations which are not of our choosing, never discern why we are apt for the gift at that particular moment or place. All such experiences expose an underlying unity of consciousness, and build all men into a totality which is integrally related to glory, but the personal reactions to them will be as various as the depths of being at which men can live. He had to himself on that particular day the museum's room of Roman inscriptions, a rich collection, and the perfection of lettering acted on him like yeast in the wine. What superb loveliness! From his depths springs the response and the acknowledgement, "Glory. It is Thou." This is. But who is Thou? Centuries ago the Hebrew consciousness knew this same path and declared the question's answer: "I am that which is." Who shall define or limit that which is the I am, the Thou? To each man his perception and acknowledgement, such as he can and will; and it will be accepted and accounted to him. Yet each plane and level of glory will need to be transcended if a man is to arrive at the End, for the lesser exaltations are rejoiced in with and through the participating self, to which there is always a return, of which there is always consciousness of different degrees. Fullest participation in glory means complete emptiness of self. No one cometh to the Father except by me, said the Lord Christ.

But we have not yet defined glory. Words open windows on eternal truths according to their universality, and what have we here? Philologically the word is exciting and any good dictionary or lexicon will uncover layers of significance. It is, for instance, such a word as 'star' or 'despair': it does not so much define as reveal, it does not confine and restrict meaning but it enlarges, unveils, discovers, blazes and thunders. It derives from the Greek δοκέω, through the roots of that verb which means to think, to suppose. What a man thinks and supposes, that which things seem to him, expresses the man himself: are his opinions mean and careless, or wise, useful, honourable? So the word expands to denote reputation, honour, that position, that renown, which is established by a man's personal beliefs and judgements. It will include his personal appearance, his external characteristics, which to some extent must stem from his opinions, and therefore will finally denote his place in society. Thus we arrive at the idea of human δόξα, glory, that which a man considers desirable, worthy, valid, to which his fellow men agree. Such glory may apply to his external possessions and state, to that which is material and costly, and to his moral and personal character. So the meanings of the word extend. But the δόξα of man is perishable, it changes, fluctuates, for what is considered honourable and worthy in one generation is scorned by the next, one man's opinions are despised by another. Reputation has no permanence. Are any opinions and beliefs valid for all time; is any condition, any attribute fixed and changeless; what is truth?

GLORY

Only a God is changeless, one whose mind is immutable, who knows to the point of omniscience because He is truth. That which makes God God is His almightiness, which itself requires absolute knowledge; His opinions, His judgements are constant, invariable, external, because God contains all truth. So here is ultimate δόξα, and we have arrived at the end beyond which there is nothing, nothing but God. The δό of God is Himself, Himself is His glory: and thus ultimately, glory can rightly be attributed to Him alone. "Why do you call me good?" asked Christ of the lawyer, "God only is good." Change 'good' into 'glorious' and the statement still stands. This is not to say that glory is God, but that God cannot be without all glory. Where is glory there is God, where God is is glory. It emanates essentially from His being. Any degree of the awareness of the reality of God in Himself, of the fact of Christ, is also a realisation of the bliss of glory. To be God's servant, child, friend, lover, is glory, indeed the only glory which has ultimate and final meaning, for it is salvation. To be accepted by God in Christ, drawn into and encircled by His glory, is man's salvation, and to be in this state is to glorify the Lord of glory. Nothing is mine, all is His, I am nothing and He is all, yet I am the voice which cries, "To Him be all glory", and it is I who must choose so to cry. O, show me Thy Glory!

Salvation, heaven, eternity, the kingdom of God, are all rays of the one indivisible light of glory; and thus in its religious significance our word has attained to fruition and completion unguessed when it began its journey up the ladder of philological use. Few words are used more often in the scriptures than glory, with great diversity of nuance, very often carrying the concomitant of light, particularly in descriptions of theophany. There is the burning bush, the shining cloud, devouring fire, the rainbow, shining brightness. From their earliest records we know that the Hebrews, like other Semitic peoples, connected light with holiness, majesty, sanctity; for them light both revealed and hid the presence of the Deity, and it was inevitable that the concepts of light and glory should become religiously almost interchangeable. This concomitance is natural to us. It is doubtful whether any place completely emptied of light could in itself ever be an imposition of glory. The velvet pools of darkness stir us by their texture only when light is there sufficient for seeing. The absence of all light can certainly be a helpful and encouraging condition for prayer, the night-hours may contribute to the ease with which we then pray, but this is because the negative state of darkness and quiet diminishes pressure on the senses, empties and quietens them, and so increases the freedom of the interior faculties. Itself the negation of light, darkness, blackness, is not a vehicle of glory: in contrast, light shines more brilliantly and is the more glorious. God dwells in light unapproachable. His infinite purity and the radiance of Godhead separate Him from all that is not Himself, but the light is ever shining in the darkness, declaring His person. The Lord's glory shines like light to the shepherds of Bethlehem, on the Mount of Transfiguration it is revealed by dazzling whiteness. And divine glory has always been seen, fleetingly but certainly, on the faces of God's lovers in all times and places. Goodness, purity and love are not the sole property of Christians, the Spirit blows where He chooses, so we catch glimpses of the reflection of glory wherever a person of any creed has arrived at some degree of union with God, through self-denial, patience and generous love of the brethren, the undeserving brethren. Whenever heaven is on the ground there will be a showing of glory. And how radiant it is with its own particular light, this glory of goodnss. One morning I turned the corner on to the promenade to be greeted with that unmistakable and rather fearful laugh of the mentally deranged, which was succeeded and enveloped by a rich shouting laugh of pure mirth and joy. There on a seat was an imbecile girl of indeterminate age with an elderly, stout grey-haired woman, as remarkable a reflection of the light of the Furnace of Charity as I have ever seen. With a visible outpouring of pure love she was entertaining, cherishing, the poor witless one, and the exuberance of hilarity aureoled the bench and rayed its quickness all around: an island of joy in the flowing stream of continual passers-by. It was worth travelling hundreds of miles to see such perfection accusing my poverty. A modern materialist advocates euthanasia for incurable imbecility, for hopeless senility, ghastly deformations, and so on; in judging life with an earthly mind he rejects heaven, thinking only of nature he ignores grace, and so assumes the responsibility of destroying its occasions and paths, of dismantling the exhibitions of its energy and truth. What shall we know of the blazing splendour of love's purest sacrifice, generated and fed by grace, if its altars are to be scientifically removed? Serve, not kill.

For everyone the process of growing up should be characterised by an extension and augmentation of the capacity to recognise splendour, greatness, brilliance, beauty under whatever forms it is displayed, in action, thought, nature and people, and to admire. This continuing development is what education should ensure, for the quick ability to admire is pre-eminently a characteristic of the human race. In all education one proceeds from the outside to the inside. It is an encouraging thing that, alongside the phenomenal growth of material possession, there is in contemporary life evidence of a deep desire for contact with the essential simplicities of the world; witness the demand for holidays in the country, for caravans, hikers' hostels and camps, the long daily journeys which workers undertake in order to live in homes on the fringe of or outside the great cities, and the millions who find nostalgic joy in out-of-town programmes on radio. This all reveals a longing to be where nature freely displays herself and conveys her gifts, for which people are appreciative and grateful, however inchoate their expression, reserved their feelings. The farm-worker who won't put his foot inside the village church and what is more, won't let his wife either, can say to me on a shining May morning, "Do you know what starts my day right? Why, I listen for the cuckoo, and when I hear him I'm proper glad." There for John is the gift and the glory in which he rejoices: and there, though he doesn't know it, is his relationship with the Creator of cuckoos who is the well-spring of bliss. Lifted above himself in his pleasure in all that the cuckoo stands for, John admires, and unconsciously participates in his Creator's eternal joy, being nearer than he knows to the declaration of the Hebrew that all nature is a revelation of God. We cannot over-rate the greatness of the contribution to mankind's knowledge of God made by the people of the Old Testament in their proclamation of His sublimity which is visible throughout the universe as He made it. "Be ye glad and rejoice forever in that which I create." Although the picture of what is disclosed as the fullness of God's glory is developed and enlarged in each successive book of the New Testament, through the characteristic spiritual insights of their writers, the Jews' adherence to God's vocation for them enabled them to asseverate for all time, in nature poetry than which there is no greater, their passionate and resolute belief in the goodness of the universe because it is created and sustained by God and must therefore disclose the fullness of His perfection.

The psalmist saw God's handiwork only in a very limited area. The world of his day was so small—play with the thought of what contemporary life would be like without any form of land transport whatsoever which is not dependent on legs! How little of our own world we could know, let alone any others, therefore how limited our knowledge of the extent, the fecundity, the diversity of nature, if it were not for modern transport, which gives us a thousand times more opportunity of marvelling at our Creator's wonders. The very modes of travel themselves contribute a means of glory. Just as the wings of a great bird lift its weight high up into the skies where it floats effortlessly in the currents of air, so we are raised aloft swiftly and surely by the power and strength of the aeroplane and like a winged creature we fly into incredible beauties of sunset or sunrise which seem to be spread before us in timeless and infinite space. On and on we are carried into immensity, the movement and the sense of it all breathing the name of God over total nature. Our dimensions to-day are immeasurably greater than those of the Hebrews.

It is impossible to force anyone to acknowledge God (though in its zeal for righteousness a church has often tried), impossible to force anyone to see glory, yet as we brood over the truth that any level and degree of glory is a reflection, however pale and subdued, of the divine effulgence, we realise that every man at some time or other draws near to God in admiration, touching the hem of His garment without knowing it. One day he will know it when he least expects what is coming.

However trivial the circumstances in which glory receives recognition, its acknowledgement is the placing of a man's hand into the hand of his unknown God and it may begin the breaking-down of estrangement and be the initial collapse of a life of rejection of the divine. It may not be known as such, yet anything near and real which claims our awed assent and admiration is actually God's creative activity: when accepted as glory, it may unconsciously be the bridge to God's person. We must not forget that glory as an image of Deity is as old as the songs of man, it can never be displaced nor lost, and is a way of communication between earth and heaven. The very sense of well-being which invariably accompanies a spontaneous act of rejoicing in any glory whatsoever is a participation in the divine Being, a spiritual drawing nearer to God even though unrecognised: that God who is endlessly communicating Himself to all creatures or they would not be, nor would even the mountains stand. Is it asking much of man to rejoice in such glory as he sees? For in the answering feeling of fruition lie the seeds of thanksgiving, and with every breath of gratitude God becomes easier to the soul, though He may still be out of sight.

The physical material world is reflective, it requires humanity to take all its wonder and rejoice in it reflectively; the vast landscapes of the universe cry out for the priestly ascendancy of man. All religious folk are priests in regard to creation, and their priesthood is exercised in this respect, by rejoicing in the glory of which we need to be constantly and vitally aware. Further, we lift up the natural world in a chalice of sacrifice and acknowledge the right of the Lord and Giver of life when we deny instincts of acquisitiveness, check tendencies to use it as an end in itself, to exploit it selfishly, to demand and use it as ours by right. We have no rights but we have a never-ceasing flow of gifts enclosed within the benefaction of the earth and its fullness, and our praise for them is the priestly offering we make. My whole being exults and cries aloud, it is good, it is good, it is good, as my senses, my mind, my emotions receive and respond to some impact of bright immensity. Do I know it or not, I am indeed rejoicing in the perfection of God,

GLORY

Creator and Lord of the goodness the truth or the beauty which is enlivening me. We are all too slow in our acknowledgements.

> *We who have seen so rich a birth*
> *Of wonders seldom rise from earth*
> *To sing of these celestial things*
> *That once have fanned us with their wings.*

Oh, do not let me misuse the experience, allow me to continue as a singing mote of joy in the beam of glory always present! Trivialities are dispersed by the growth of a habit of praise and by it the soul is poised in peace and calm. Yet God forbid that the careful rendering of thanks which it is our duty to make for what we enjoy should mean that we are continually drawing attention to our gratitude, forcing ourselves to express it in a self-conscious manner, publicly enthroning God in every pleasure. This is to bring Him down to the level of a bookmark. And we who know ourselves to be sons of God and heirs of the kingdom of heaven have to learn to pass on beyond joy in the world to joy in the world's Creator, from the offering of thanks for created beauty to thanksgiving to God for Himself, for the inexpressible glory of His Majesty. So we prepare ourselves to receive from Him the gift of thanksgiving not only for but in Himself, if and as He wills: but this is His mystery. But whatever happens, we must not be waylaid. The Christian way is the exploration and the following of the double track of affirmation and negation in respect of every aspect of life and living which can confront us. The search for God, our longings for fulfilment, the pursuit of perfection, is this never-ending problem and process of resolving the tensions between these two opposing laws. All that life holds is presented to us and we accept, we affirm, we use, we enjoy; then, responding to divine pressure and to spiritual light, we refuse, deny, leave aside, learning to live by grace as well as, even more than, by nature; all so that finally we may be free, unfettered, whole, and able therefore to possess all because we are possessed by God in love. This is the rhythm of the new law, the new life. The body is for the Lord, and the Lord for the body, that is, the world is for God, and for me as far as I am all for God. This is what Christ called the narrow way which leads to life, in which he who perseveres to the end shall be saved. The end, the salvation, the way itself, is glory.

SUFFERING

Glory. So let us bless and adore God the source of all glory. Impossible, she said, not when my son is cruelly ill. Why should he have to suffer like this? I am blacked out with anxiety, I cannot say a prayer or go to church.

'Glory? he said, Wonder?'

Nuts, the world is a lousy place, sick to the heart.

Even though we cannot cease to believe that the glory of the inexpressible Being fills the heavens and is shown on earth, none of us can be deaf to the accumulation of abuse hurled at this life. It stinks, it yawns black and murderous; cruelty, lust and malice cover it like unchecked floods, greed for power is enthroned, falsities win crowns. Bodily pains, mental blackness in which a man crouches less a man than a beast, grey horrors, pursuing fears—all are acknowledged, for all that is here. Some have known the weight of woe since childhood, know it as a companion so near and smothering that one day it provokes suicide. Others refuse to face its force and seek to withdraw from the struggle of adjustment, closing the pores of the soul to suffering as I may close my eyes to the mangled body in the road. Without much difficulty they, assuming blamelessness, build a refuge-citadel of fancied delicacy and rectitude, of self-vindication and real insensibility. Refuse everything which does not minister to comfort and ask nothing which can disturb it, becomes their rule. But the cry that is universal down the ages from all docile hearts which love, which serve, which are alert to greatness, is why, why, why? Even more general, perhaps, and certainly more imperative, is the poignant question, what must I do? For life is to be lived and when I am assailed by dark agony, how can I care about glory. When all my being is twisted in fetters of anguish, then where is light? empty of everything but drear dullness, how can there be joy?

> *My heart was never strong*
> *And cannot cope for long*
> *Against the sum of wrong*
> *Encompassing.**

I cannot cope.

I shall not begin or want to cope if either I refuse the sorry situation or blame anyone else for it. What must I do? is answered first by "Do not blame God". People do this, most freely: they blame Him for the accident, the cancer, the war, and then make this the excuse for dropping Him out of their picture of reality; for them He no longer counts, is no more within the focus of relationship. God, they say, is creator and so it is His fault that the world is dark, full of jagged rocks, storms, pests, famines, disease, obscenities, fear. Of course, this the world is, but that is only half of the picture, and the other half of the diptych glows with all that we enjoy, all that is pure, lovely, universally praised. So, we must accede, the world could be worse, it could be all black, wholly conditioned to evil, which is hell; and of course it could, we think, be better, unable to contain evil: which is heaven. But it is neither, it is earth winning its way to heaven, and as such it has to be accepted as the best, surest and most blessed way here and now for us men. It is impossible to accept this terrestrial life as it is,

* *Death, lovely little child*, E. H. W. Meyerstein.

blaming no creator, unless we agree that not only is it good, but it is as we would have it. Of course the rat-infested tenement in an industrial slum is not good, nor the lives of crime it can engender, but don't blame God, blame human cupidity. Try tracing to their causes the situations and happenings which you so readily describe as intolerably calamitous, and you will find few that do not arise from ill-will, disobedience to divine laws and human reasoning, from ignorance ultimately culpable. For all of this we cannot grumble at God; a tendency which when we are in trouble is more frequent than we like to recognise or acknowledge. 'It isn't fair.' We should be intolerably inhuman were we without man's power to choose either good or evil, this way or that. Surely that is what claims our wonder and, if you like, our blame, the freedom of will with which God has dowered and trusted us, which produces not only the ghastly breakdowns in human relationships with all their consequent sufferings but which also impels people to devote themselves to the alleviation of misery without any consideration of personal gain: altruistic devotion shown both in public service and in private reparation and penance. Whom do we 'blame' for all that is good, all that is lovely, all that is exalting?

The one and only ground for accepting the world as God has made it is actually not because His law ordains it but because by unique Incarnation He entered this creation, and within it accepted, embraced and lived just such a life as is common to all. Once in time and in place Deity lived historically, as man, and could God-man be anything less than perfect man? Not if He were also truly God. We stand, kneel, prostrate before the mystery of this miracle, which finally is the only miracle; no serious mind can dwell reverently upon it without being enlarged by wonder and awe, even if it fails to accept. Because we adhere to this stupendous belief we have our criterion to which we turn for reference in every problem; so now we ask, what did the perfect man, what did God the Son incarnate think and what did He do about suffering? Is He indifferent, does He disregard, does He blame, condemn, oppose? We must ask Him what was His mind on this problem, and find His answer for those who cry in the bitterness of misery, "Tell me why, what is the use, where is there any rest, where light or joy?" For surely when He was a man He had to answer these questions, and the light of the perfect life of Jesus Christ is the only one which will illuminate the world's dark paths of pain. It follows that His life recorded in the Gospels remains our primary study all our days.

From birth onwards, the Lord of the world accepted a life marked by limitations and deprivations. He lived ordinarily, in no sheltered precious existence, with one peculiarity, which to-day is often advanced as an excuse for abberations, defects, maladjustments. 'Not like other children' is now advanced as a justification for delinquencies. Well, the Jesus of Nazareth was not like other children, in that His mother had a secret. Perhaps, too, He was unique in having a mother who was perfect: in that He was not ordinary in our sense. Yet later He cried aloud that He was so intensely and universally a part of ordinariness that all women were His mother. As we trace the circumstances of His life we acknowledge their poverty of privilege; there was nothing He could claim as His peculiar property. Homelessness and exile on his account were thrust upon his family, conditions which by their prevalency to-day stir contemporary social conscience. He belonged to a subject race which was isolated in culture by its peculiar religious claims, tolerated by its rulers but inevitably misunderstood, disliked by its neighbours for its pride and self-consciousness in being the chosen people of God, aloof in its belief in its theocracy: not a comfortable nation. Home rule was not His birthright, nor social position, intellectual opportunities, leisure, nor the choice of occupation, those favours of wealth and ideal government. There was nothing abject or penalising in Jesus' manner of life, it was simply that which has always been the lot of millions of workers of inferior status throughout the world. If our term 'under-privileged' would not have been justly applied to Him in His day, it is certain that one in His position, neither then nor to-day, could claim no possession, position or privilege which would lift him much above the have-nots. All this He accepts and, by accepting, allows it to make no difference whatsoever to His development, His perfection, His fulfilment. For when Jesus abruptly terminates His thirty-odd years of ordinary private life to make public His almost incredible claims on the world, He shows that no limitations whatsoever, no handicaps of inheritance, location, nature, personality, and no opposition, can prevent a man from fulfilling any vocation, however unlikely, if he knows that it is God's will for him. The power of a true vocation is displayed when anyone responds to his individual and particular inner light, follows the star which he perhaps alone can see, chooses at whatever cost to obey the beckoning hand which points to the path he must take. So it is that out of an environment of sheer ordinariness there steps at the moment of grace on to the stage of the world He who is to make for Himself immense and awful claims, and on His followers demands so extraordinary and compelling that they have been talked about ever since, and have changed human history beyond human computation. That is what from external observation any rational person is bound to acknowledge. Because it is necessary for us to measure our circumstances by His, we have looked at the outward shape of Christ's life only so that we may assure ourselves that He has not, as it were, any tricks up His sleeve which will enable Him to manipulate for His own ends the inexorable conditions which life imposes on all of us; for which, so many like Job curse God (usually without that intellectual integrity and spiritual agony which were Job's in his search for the reason why). Jesus was, as man, a man of ordinariness, who felt, faced and carried, the frets, the perplexities, the pains of nature on every level of being: if He had not been so, we could not look to Him as our pattern and example. That example displays how little He is bound, constrained or limited, by the human milieu which He accepts, how powerfully He is its master.

What is meant by this condition of acceptance? It is not a dull resignation, which can be little more than a defence mechanism doping the feelings and inducing a sense of safety, possibly even of self-righteousness. It is not a take-it-at-any-price attitude in order to buy repose and inertia, nor a thoughtless acquiescence. Acceptance carries an implication of acting, of taking hold, of a positive use, even of donation. Its root-verb is one of those exciting words which contain paradox, for it can mean both give and take. Christian acceptance must of course be a matter of discrimination and knowledge. I accept this situation, place, person even though I am aware of defect, distortion, wrong, malevolence, because I know that, for the present at least, it is not my concern or calling to change what is offensive; but it may, of course, be someone else's job. I do not close my mind or my senses to the undesirable nor pretend that I am not hurt, but I receive it and spin around it the threads of endurance, patience, compassion with sorrow. "Render unto Caesar," said Christ: and so He did, and so often must we: though any nationalist may have to refuse to accept and to render, burning with zeal to throw off Caesar's claims, because in fact this is the very thing he has to do. But

SUFFERING

Jesus' vocation was not to be a revolutionary racial leader, so He accepted Caesar, as He accepted without lament the limitations of place, time and society, the effects of accident, tyranny, power, above all the multiform complexities of human nature. "He shall not strive, nor cry . . . till he send forth judgement unto victory."*

To what did Jesus Christ show active hostility, where physical defiance, where rebellion against convention? We are given a description of one occasion when He refused to accept common custom and usage, when He made a sudden attack in the courts of the Jews' most holy Temple, with such whirlwind violence that single-handed He drove out the offending salesmen, together with their sheep and oxen, threw over the money-changers' tables scattering all their piles of coins and tallies. Noise, confusion, shouting, banging, running feet and scudding hooves, with one angry man as the cause. The Christ defied blasphemy. And harshly, fiercely, He expressed His indignation and anger with false religiosity, with spiritual blindness built on pride, with personal vanity, when He uncovered the vices of His national leaders and religious guides. Fearlessly He sent stinging messages to a corrupt governor. He denounced faithlessness and lack of trust in His followers, but how notably gentle and patient, full of forbearance He was, with the faults and frailties of the band of apostles whom He knew so intimately. He knew in truth everything about human nature, and He allows for all its weaknesses. What He will not tolerate is self-love, hypocrisy, a deliberate refusal to receive knowledge of God, which is the choice of darkness instead of light. Whoever elects to sin against the Holy Spirit is not accepted. What saddens our Lord is not the tide of common suffering which beats against the shores of all human life, from

* Math. 12, 19:20.

which there seems no escape, but the refusal to receive the safety, the security, the comfort which He yearns to give. How often would I gather you to me and show you how to live, give you the power to live, but you would not, He cries; come to me, I will give you rest. But no, we want that only on our terms, not His. To our Lord, men seem like sheep who without a shepherd have no notion as to where to pasture, what paths to take. How large the world, how vast the multitudes, how few to show them where lies their hope, their blessedness, their peace, to reveal the things which belong in place of those which are alien, discordant, distracting: that is what makes Him weep, what stirs His compassion.

We are trying to look at the God-Man as He walks the ways of life which we all must travel and to put ourselves alongside Him in ordinary circumstances. Does He ever ask the questions we ask about suffering of any sort, pain of any kind? So much of our conversation is on what we have to put up with, on all the varying trials of life; how did they affect Him and what does He say? He says almost nothing at all. In particular there is no condemnation of earthquakes, famines and wars, which are part of temporal existence to be endured until the Kingdom of God shall come; in fact a mounting succession of such calamities is, He says, a sign of hope, that the time of delivery is at hand when God shall be all in all. There is no condemnation of sickness as an evil to be feared and resisted in the way that the power of Satan, prince of this world, is to be feared and resisted. There is a warning against connecting a man's illness with his own individual sins or his parents', and against thinking that violent death is any sign of, or punishment for, sin. He overcomes disease and death, not with an anger which burns to eliminate what offends the Father (as in the desecration of the Temple) but by love. Christ's overflowing compassion constrains Him to relieve physical suffering whenever He is asked to do this: it is noteworthy that He rarely offers a cure unless there is first a request; the healing of the paralytic at Bethesda's miraculous pool and the restoration of the widow's dead son at Nain are exceptions. There were many invalids at the pool whom He did not cure, many other funeral processions He let go on their way. But when folks lame, blind, deaf, dumb, impotent, incurable, come with faith and desire, He heals them all. Faced with crowds who are hungry, individuals outworn with grief, sufferers in mind and body, Christ's torrent of pity leaps to succour and to comfort. He has power to heal: the sign and the demand of His gospel, His kingdom, His revelation of God, is love, and love serves. So, one of the signs of the validity of His gospel and the new kingdom will be the healing powers of His disciples as they go out on their mission. There are some occasions when He dispersed His friends' fears by overriding natural forces, for inevitably His love for them is such that He would prevent any suffering whilst He the Bridegroom is with them. What is the measure of love? Eagerness, generosity, the extent of self-forgetfulness with which it serves, the delight with which it gives. A boundless love will serve, Christ said, to the limit of death, and many noble men and women have so served. But there is no indication at all that when He used His power to overcome disease, even death, Christ was driven by an anger or an impetuous desire to eliminate what was an affront to His Father and opposition to His will, but rather by perfection of sympathy, which is the property of perfect love, by His burning desire to give peace, to restore order, to provide fullness of life for the children of God. His widely-used powers of healing were signs of His mission, of His gospel and of His divine authority, above all, a revelation of love.

There comes a day, a moment of intense gravity, when Jesus

does speak of suffering, but it is of suffering related to Himself. As a wise mother who, always watchful of her child's development, knows when by some timely words it is ready to receive an intimation of some forthcoming experience which she hopes it will not resist or find alarming, so Christ must have waited for the moment when His disciples were psychologically and spiritually ready to accept the idea that their Master is destined for extraordinary suffering. How closely He must have observed them, that He could judge when to make this harsh, bitter revelation in such a manner that they will not be scared into flight, like birds at the sound of a shotgun. He began, say all the evangelists, to teach them that He, the Son of Man, must suffer many things, finally must die a criminal's death. Peter's immediate reaction to this appalling announcement—and no doubt he is saying only what all are thinking—is a refusal to tolerate such possibilities, which brings upon him the sternest rebuke he has ever received from the Lord. Yet surely this announcement of violent and final suffering for their Jesus is one against which they would inevitably rebel. They had only to look at Him to feel that it was impossible to connect Him with pain, He who wherever He went relieved it. They looked at, they touched, they heard, perfection personalised; could such a person ever be marred by suffering? Christ's external appearance and physical qualities must have been outstandingly attractive and powerful, compelling attention and admiration. Immense vitality would vibrate from the perfect balance and poise of physique and radiant health, the effect as well as the expression of the perfection of His will and His disciplined mind, of His unified emotions and of the clarity of His interior vision; all this issuing from total union with His Father. He could call His followers to perfection only because He himself mirrored it as He knew it in the Father, for "I and the Father are one". The unity, purity and transparency of His being must have bestowed on Him bodily nobility, splendour of face, intensity of eyes. "If thine eye be single thy whole body shall be full of light." It would be wise if we could abolish all those pictures of an emasculated powerless static Christ which gaze palely at nothing from books and pictures of pious shops. None of the sicknesses or physical disabilities common to most people could ever have touched Him. He was strong and resilient enough to continue tireless through day after day of arduous life, days like a river filled with water forever flowing onward; preaching in public, teaching in private, ministering to crowds who want His healing touch, walking the roads and the paths of Palestine as He takes His proclamation of the kingdom of God from village to village, synagogue to synagogue. Wherever He went there were crowds, drawn to Him by the astonishing miracles which were signs of His stature, drawn by His compelling personality and the vision of a new way of life which it presented. Crowds everywhere, days without leisure, so it was His custom to steal hours from the night for communion with God in the silent country places. Yet always the Christ appeared tireless, confident, secure, responding to every sort of situation and emergency, including arguments with an enlarging opposition party of the nation's *élite* which steadily increased in antipathy, even to attempted assaults on His person. As the disciples saw their Lord always the master of the situation, always quietly in control, they could not envisage Him as losing the final game, being trapped, caught, tormented, killed. No wave of ultimate defeat could break over Him, surely He could escape? Why not?

Yet of course they knew all the references in their scriptures not only to 'He that should come' as the Messiah, but also to the suffering servant who was a vicarious victim offered on behalf of God's chosen, but sinful, people, One mighty to save, but redeeming through suffering. Deep within their national consciousness was the world's fullest and noblest conception of religious sacrifice, grounded upon concentrated attention to the spiritual insights of men dedicated to the service of God, developed through centuries of symbolic action and practice. Think of the significance of the great liturgical wealth inherited by every Jew. Yet how much of what we ourselves unthinkingly accept and adhere to in theory fails to be worked out in literal practice or seen as factual reality, how slow we are to grasp the implications of articles of belief. We have no right to censure the disciples for obtuseness; that we must leave to the Lord. "O foolish men and slow of heart."

Christ lived with the thought of suffering. Let us with awe and reverence, profoundly aware of our nescience, try to look at the soul of our Incarnate God. We know for a fact that by His twelfth year Jesus, by His essential union with His Father, has a knowledge of the majesty of His unique vocation, and throughout the preparation period of those quiet working years at Nazareth, there would have been a continuous deepening both of self-knowledge and of the Father's will. Like the sun rising at dawn without upheaval, clangour or force, yet whose coming is inevitable, final and triumphant, Christ arrived in the sky of history to reveal this destiny, fully conscious that He is the Messiah, the long-expected anointed servant of God who is the saviour and king of the people (albeit He is to give a new value to the titles and fill with a new spiritual meaning the Jewish conception, which was limited, material and earthly). From His study of, and long brooding over, the prophecies, He would have applied to Himself and the role of the Messiah

SUFFERING

the term of the suffering servant and its evaluation. In all the religious literature of the world there is no writing so inspired as the passages in the book of Isaiah, which describe this enigmatical person; such is the simplicity, the poignancy, paradox, and nobility, that one is inclined to cry, impossible, this beauty blinds me. Read them, read them aloud, these glorious passages which are the climax of all Old Testament prophecy, found in Chapters 42, 49, 50, 52 and 53. (Why are these not read again and again from our lecterns instead of the dull irrelevancies under which we often groan?)

> My servant: I gave my cheek to the smiters, I hid not my face from shame and spitting. He was despised and rejected of men, a man of sorrows and acquainted with grief,
> As one from whom men hide their faces.
> He was despised and we esteemed Him not,
> We esteemed Him stricken, smitten by God and afflicted.
> He was wounded,
> He was bruised,
> Upon Him was the chastisement.
> He was oppressed, He was afflicted,
> Yet he opened not His mouth.
> Like a lamb led to the slaughter
> Like a sheep before its shearers is dumb
> So He opened not His mouth.
> By oppression and judgement He was taken away,
> He was cut off out of the land of the living, stricken for the transgressions of my people.
> They made His grave with the wicked
> Altho' He had done no violence
> Yet it was the will of the Lord to bruise Him, to put Him to grief.

He poured out His soul to death.

Yet He bore the sin of many and made intercession for transgressors.

We to-day, with the Gospels before us, look back from the real to the picture, from the substance to the shadow, from truth to symbol. We hold, as it were, the finished article in our hands and consider the process: but Jesus the Person had to look forward. He had to recognise in ancient writings the poetry and picture which described Himself, and as their subject He had to fulfil their details. How did He know? If only we could see and understand but a little of the purity of the Lord's intellect which could penetrate the veils of prophecy to the archetype, of the clarity and transparency of His vision which recognised and swiftly embraced everything which was relevant to the will of His Father. All through His hidden years the conviction of the inherent necessity of those pains and tormenting death, which would complete His life of obedience to that will, would have deepened until it so dominated His whole conception of His mission that it became the prevailing element of the teaching which He strove to give his intimate followers. He had to persuade them to realise this truth, that what the Son of Man was to do, or rather, what was to be done to Him, would have infinitely greater power than anything which He came to say. That which He was about to do was to give Himself to suffering: I, if I be lifted up, will draw all men: first must the Son of Man suffer. Must: He shall be, He is, He must be, delivered into the hands of men who will torment and kill. So Jesus said, dwelling repeatedly upon this necessity for the suffering servant. No doubt he would often ask them, "Have you understood all these things?" No, not at the time did they understand, but there is no doubt as to the mind of the early church. Saint Peter, within a few days, within a few weeks of the day of Pentecost, proclaimed that "the things which God foreshowed by the mouth of all the prophets, that His Christ should suffer, He thus fulfilled." Saint Paul declared in His defence before King Agrippa that His own preaching was no more than that of the prophets, how that Christ must first suffer. The synoptic writers recognised and accepted the paramount importance of the Passion, for their narratives are consistent in the large amount of space devoted to it. In fact, in the inspired order of the New Testament writings, we find a crescendo of understanding of Christ's sufferings in their central place in the drama of redemption and therefore in the whole display of creation, until the man Jesus who was crucified in their own time was declared to be the Lamb slain before the foundation of the world, from all eternity. If this is not so, the Passion has no universal and timeless meaning.

This immediate centralising of Christ's sufferings in the heart of apostolic preaching and writing could only be the result of our Lord's own behaviour and attitude towards them; they were accepted, embraced, taken possession of, because they had for Him meaning, purpose, and were a way of fulfilment. Why, the very beginning of His public ministry was a prolonged adventure of suffering, about which the disciples knew only because He told them on one of the rare occasions when He disclosed to them the intimate workings of His interior religious experience. When, we wonder, had He shared with them the epic of His weeks of solitary life in the rocky and mountainous countryside? In a rapt state of exaltation, on fire with holy dedication and alight with the consciousness of being ready for His Father's work, Jesus went from His baptism into solitude with the swiftness of the straight flight of an eagle to its eyrie, without thought of bodily comfort or even of necessities. Eagerly He would fast, He would watch, nights as well as days would He give to prayer, for those conditions gave Him what His whole being cried out for, communion with God and the vision of God by which He lived. Later devotional writers like to linger over the physical hardships and make much of His bodily suffering, but although they were present, He would not have made much of them, they were not greater than those endured by generations of explorers, scientific travellers and missionaries. Rapt in direct experience of His Father's love and will, Christ could ignore bodily claims. But He had come into this world not to live the life of heaven but of men, and as man He naturally found that when He was stretched to the limits of self-forgetfulness His interior silence and His absorption with His Father's business were invaded by cravings, desires, and physical demands clamouring for satisfaction. Desperately hungry, worn out and weary, there came into consciousness the idea that He could satisfy the valid needs of His body by using His power over matter. Perhaps this power had just been made particularly clear to Him by the control He had established over the wild creatures who, notes Saint Mark, shared His retreat, for although He was defenceless, He had received no injury, although alone, had perhaps enjoyed a sympathy in their companionship. Who can say what development of religious experience revealed to Christ His inherent power to control matter and the powers of nature: 'I could have turned the stones into bread.' But our Lord had the strength of will to refuse to employ any spiritual power for the satisfaction of His bodily wants, choosing to remain dependent upon the grace of His Father's will. To fast is good, to feast is good, both are necessary; so, bodily life is to be accepted and lived to the fullness of good nature, but always as both dependent upon and serving the life of the spirit, of supernature; for this is the essential and that which is eternal and our home. And, trusting to the essential, placing His confidence in it, Our Lord refused to work a miracle for His natural benefit. But we must not belittle the strength of the physical pangs of hunger, the strong demands of His body, which Jesus had to resist in this temptation to abandon His dependence upon God by breaking the fast according to His own will. Christ had all the normal physical appetites of a man, not only for food, and all of them to to be dealt with, every prick and urge of natural life. It is hard for us to accept Him as a man tempted in all points as we are. Perhaps it was after a disciple asked a question about the control of carnal cravings that our Lord exposed to them the reality of His own temptations.

The second temptation follows logically; if a man actually receives power to live from a spiritual nourishment derived from doing God's will, over and above the natural sources of food and drink, why not live entirely in the spirit, trusting to God to take all care? Could this be the necessary revelation of the coming of the kingdom? Mighty signs, miracles which defy normal nature, will surely demonstrate the power of God and the greatness of His anointed one, so, prove God to the anxious world by disregarding the body and all the laws which govern it, even gravity, demonstrate the primacy of spirit by a gigantic gesture of abandonment which none can fail to see. But who ordained the laws of the world in which we live, and to whose glory would it be if they were set aside? Not by the way of miracle is virtue proved and taught, nor union with

God displayed and maintained. Christ showed us how profound was His struggle for knowledge as to the ways and means by which He should reveal His Father to men, what an agony of mental strife He suffered between the opposite ways of evangelisation proposed for His acceptance. Which is the right way, the true way? The purer and stronger the desire to do God's will, the more intense and costly will be the resolution to make the right decision: but what is it? I know, says Christ, for in this temptation I was presented with two courses of action, either one decisive, one ruling out the other, and I also knew the agony of, 'shall I, or shan't I, this or that?' If truly man, Jesus knew the tension produced by the ambivalence of our essential creatureliness on one hand and our place in providence on the other, neither of which can be displaced; although the harmony which is being resolved through this tension is itself a mode of union with God in and by love. But tension hurts.

You, my Jesus, are incomprehensibly pure, flawless, untouched by any fleck of sin, you could never have known in any part of your self-consciousness, in the depths or the fringe, the smallest stirring of delight in personal power, the slightest suggestion of satisfaction in your superb strengths of personality, nor a momentary occupation with the self for self's sake. No movement of self-satisfaction could ever have cracked your soul's union with God. "I do always the will of my Father", so, no energy was ever deflected from glorying in Him. Yet one of my temptations was, Christ told His disciples, a struggle with pride. All the whole world, all peoples, kindred, tongues, all whom He had come to call to blessedness, all could be manipulated by Him into goodness, all governed by Him in a rule of peace, for "all power is given to me in Heaven and earth". To me, 'Come,' insinuates an ingratiating inner voice,

SUFFERING

'take this kingdom which you have been sent to claim, take the power and the glory in a way which all people will understand; you are worthy, you have the right to worthship, so, be king. At least take the power and then the glory shall be God's: is not this the design of your Messianic kingdom?' But Jesus knew the way that it should come: "not by might, nor by power, but by my spirit" was the prophecy. So He refused to accept, to acknowledge as worthy or true the suggestion of earthly power dominated by His manhood, possible though it could be. He accepted, rather, the truth that before its visible impact is seen by the world, the kingdom of God must first come within the souls of men. Silently, almost unnoticed, like the smallest of seeds which yet grows into a strong branched tree simply by complying with the laws of its organic life, the new kingdom will emerge, has emerged, and Christ as its Lord is to be a suffering servant, without the customary splendour of a temporal king. In unfathomable humility He accepted the reversal of majesty, because that was the Father's will, His glory. Nowhere in Christ's soul was there any resting-place for self-possession, the only assertion, acknowledgement and declaration was that of the all-embracing power and permeation of the Father. But the interior struggle, long and continuous, to maintain Himself in obedience and dependence, to see His future in the light not of expediency, but of the Father's will, what did this cost the Son? We tend to dwell on the amazing beauty of His soul and on the holiness in which there is never a momentary acceptance of any thrust of self-assumption, self-assertion, self-glorification, and we forget the price of His wholeness. We also forget the wounds which must have been inflicted by the ugliness, the filth, the stench of the sin which proposed itself in these temptations, because we ourselves are seldom sensitive to its horror. Battered and crushed in His interior faculties as well as worn from weeks of conditions of unusual physical severity, Jesus came near to the point of death. No human help was available in the desert and therefore angelic aid was sent, heavenly ministry came to support the prince of Life, or so the Lord must have told His disciples. They would recall this, three short yet long years later, when at the close of Christ's final death-struggle with temptation in Gethsemane they saw the angel ministering to Him: a service which gave Him His embrace of the cross. The pattern is repeated.

Most people get what they want if they will it enough, get what they ultimately live for, they shape their lives to it. Did Christ live to suffer? From beginning to end His life is patterned with suffering, received from all the zones of experience through which it can come to humanity. Said John Donne superbly, "Christmas Day and His Good Friday are but the evening and the morning of one and the same day." It is, we notice, the morning which holds the Passion: if anyone objects that Christ's life held no long martyrdom of year upon year of physical suffering such as some people endure, surely it is undeniable that interior suffering is a far heavier burden than physical pain and disabilities, that mental blackness and doubt, emotional fears, spiritual anguish and unquiet, are burdens more overwhelming than bodily ills however crippling and prolonged. But, Christ Jesus shows us, no natural calamity, no external assaults, no force of misery and imposition of evil can penetrate and defile the soul which maintains itself in love and withholds consent of the will. The almost unendurable test is there, in love: and then, the burden is light: so He says.

SUFFERING

*He who does not experience sufferings in this vale of sorrow
Knows nothing of good things
Nor has he tasted of love
For suffering is the dress of lovers.*

So sang the Carmelite nuns of Beas, who knew. But have we by now lost all sight of glory?

SACRIFICE

Father of Truth
Behold your Son
Who makes atoning sacrifice

Glory has been declared, but we know that in effect we live in the midst of horror, fear, pain, which blot it out. Suffering is suffering, not glory, and can two opposites be contained in one and the same activity, can they abide together in one experience? Can there be a super-imposition or super-impregnation, a transfiguration so that each is maintained in its essential quality, each being required for the other? Our Lord seems to suggest this, even in the very little which He says about suffering: "Ought not Christ to have suffered these things and to enter into His glory?" Ought not, wasn't it necessary: equally then, wasn't it God's will? Continuing this sequence, God's will is a glory, and cannot be otherwise, since His will is Himself and Himself is His glory. Consequently, life is devoid of meaning if there is no sense and sight of glory. But it was after their accomplishment that Christ linked His sufferings with glory, not when He was first disclosing to the disciples their necessity. When first He impelled their thoughts forward to that impossible, that incredible end to His life, there was no suggestion at all that it meant an hour of golden glory. There was, of course, one actual display, a kind of preview of the paradox, when on Mount Tabor Christ and the two saints of the Old Covenant spoke of His death whilst they were all transfigured in a dazzling glory. When Christ instructed His disciples in the necessity of His passion He spoke also of its sequel, the resurrection. "The Son of Man must suffer, be killed, and after three days, rise again." But 'to rise again' was so far outside the norm of experience that the apostles' minds barely registered this strange statement, certainly did not seize upon it as a contingent consequence of death, issuing in transcendent glory. In fact, Christ scarcely uses that word 'glory' and never apart from His Father or heaven. He is occupied with living His earthly life, which for Him is a progress of suffering to death, and it is only when all has been consummated that He declares that this has been the essential preliminary to glory; a state which He then asserts, takes for granted, assumes as if by right. And it is not until they have had their part in the experience of Christ's sufferings by actually witnessing them, and have received through every normal avenue of knowledge the fact of His resurrection, that the apostles speak of glory. Then they cannot stop speaking of it, the apostolic writings resound with its declaration. Those Palestinian men had known Christ in His humanity as we never can, for three wonderful years they have lived in closest companionship with Him to whom they would have applied every epithet of respect, esteem, homage and love and still have fallen short of describing His perfection; yet it was only after they had lost Him in the body and entered into spiritual union with Him risen and ascended into the heavenlies, that they actually apprehended within their own experiences the truth of the relation between suffering and glory, discovering that blessedness does really come, as He declared, through mourning. It was the cross and passion which opened the eyes, the hearts and the minds of the disciples to the whole mystery of redemption, it will be through suffering that we also learn it, learn life.

> *And here, in dust and dirt, O here*
> *The lilies of His love appear.*

Perhaps we doubt whether the historic pains of Jesus Christ, endured centuries ago, however noble, sacrificial and appealing they may be, can have anything to do with the ordinary troubles of our prosaic lives. How do we relate His Passion to ourselves, make it not only a vital reality but also vitally integral and effective for our glory? It is inevitably of ourselves we must finally think, of what we personally are to believe and do, for we all have to cope with this world and its life, be the heart strong or otherwise: though one copes with energy, another with lethargy. If Jesus' pains were not simply His concern once upon a time but are of actual use to us now, we must be sure that we know them. We have to look at them with not less concentration than people show as they watch a tragedy on the screen; and we have to see them not only with eyes but with minds, not only with ears but with hearts, enclosing these interior faculties within faith which is as necessary to the spirit as air to the body. As we cannot now spread our attention over all the successive scenes of Christ's passion, let us concentrate upon its prologue, that scene which is displayed, as it were, before the curtain rises upon the full drama. No episode of the Passion has a greater mobilisation of agony than the hour in the garden of Gethsemane yet none is so readily accessible to our understanding and actual experience, for the more we analyse it the more it displays all the modes and categories of our own sufferings. Despite our undoubted spiritual insufficiency and blindness, we will, with whatever humility and reverence we can summon, try with all meekness to think, feel and pray with Jesus in that garden, approaching Him interiorly as we watch Him externally. Though that upon which we meditate happened once in a particular hour and place it is also happening now, this minute, all over the world, in countless suffering souls. May God the Spirit give us light without which we can see nothing of His truth: and love will follow.

The sufferings of Jesus begin in the upper room where He has spent the evening. There He has just given to His embryo church its own peculiar rite, that astounding confluence of spirit and matter, of heavenly and earthly, of eternity and time: a wonder unique in history and experience which yields treasure at every fresh exploration: a chord of such fullness that no one ear can compass all its harmonies and vibrations in one hearing. Christ's vision of the rite of the Last Supper, His creation and establishment of this supreme religious operation, would heighten His every faculty, stretch every sensitive nerve, demand all spiritual energy, and while exalting would also drain the Lord's system of natural vitality. Any artist knows the condition of weary emptiness when strength and power have been drained away by a prolonged activity of high creation. Besides the institution of the Eucharist there are other strange acts and words, not to be understood at the time: what do the disciples make of the feet-washing, of the odd sign to Judas? Far beyond their immediate comprehension are the mysteries and half-lights of the symbolic acts and veiled words of this last family-meal, but they surely stir and deepen the obscure fears and dismaying apprehension which fill the disciples. Dark dread envelops them all. For how long had the Master known that one of His chosen band was plotting His betrayal with those who had, with increasing virulence, become

His avowed antagonists? One who could read men's hearts as plainly as a face is seen in a mirror perhaps carried the precognition that this *dénouement* was inevitable even from the moment of selection. The warning had been given to the company when Christ told them the parable of the wheat and tares growing together until the end of time. Though to know in advance would eliminate surprise, it would not diminish His grief for the apostasy, and His pain at such travesty of love.

So, it is in sadness and obscurity that Jesus and His few friends walk out of the city to the quiet garden, well known to them as a place for their talk and prayer. Nightfall with its growing silence underlines gravity; surely there must have been a sense of finality communicated from the Lord to His disciples? The perfect Son must already have said farewell to His mother, if not in one definite heart-rending moment then in some pause of mutual understanding and acceptance; for, from the knowledge which is the fruit of true love, each would have been aware of the other when impending separation was near. For the last time those two have communicated in trustful joy of each other, and now Jesus adds to His own pain the inclusion of His mother's, and He gives His to her. Yet in her perfection she would accept what Her Son wished her to accept and thus give to Him her energy of strengthening compassion: this we cannot doubt, though it means no lessening of pain. His mother, yes: but how will the disciples react? He knows: they will all, all forsake Him, run away, forswear. Sick with foreboding they already are, for what depresses and gnaws at courage more than prescience that catastrophe is approaching when there is ignorance of its details? We do not need to possess the Gaelic faculty of 'the sight' to have experienced now and again some heavy apprehension of disaster, of an unwel-

SACRIFICE

come intrusion and of calamity advancing to wreck our peace; such an oppression weighs more relentlessly when we are ignorant of the cause. Those heavy-hearted men must feel with their Lord as though they are walking along a precipice in the gloom of thick night, that at some point the path must end, and what then? They are all trapped in danger.

Why does Jesus want His friends to be with Him now, the men who have, He said, been with him through all His temptations? The Gospel narratives make it very clear that Jesus was remarkably independent of men's society; He gave but He did not require to receive, for His interior communion with His Father sufficed. Even in His boyhood His consciousness of a unique relationship with the Heavenly Father was the dominant and controlling force. Although His overflowing love and charity impel Him to mix with all men, freely, and accessibly, with gracious eagerness spending Himself for their comfort, yet personally He does not need them; though for the accomplishment of His mission each one is necessary, even Judas to whom the Lord is so courteous. Between the Man Jesus and His brethren there is a separating gulf, the deep gulf of that inner silence where He dwelt with the Father. Not that He was self-sufficient but, rather, He was God-sufficient. Yet now in this hour of anguish Jesus underlines His human nature—our nature, by wanting the presence of His most familiar friends. Where is He to find refuge, where a covering from the avalanche of evil which His spirit recognises as advancing upon Him, an avalanche which spells obliteration, where if not in their love? If malice and misunderstanding overwhelm us, instinctively we run to a friend, to a home, for solace and sympathy. Jesus wants the solace of His friends: and they are with Him. But He departs from the group to go on into the heart of the olive-grove with the chosen three who had seen His transfiguration in glory on Mount Tabor, for, remembering that, surely they would now support His transfiguration in torment? I cannot bear this terrible aloneness, I cannot face what is coming to me, be with me now in my agony. He actually tells them that He is filled with dread and woe as never before, and He begs for the sympathy of their company. Loneliness is a very profound pain: yet so much of our spiritual growth is attained by bearing things alone until breaking-point is reached: if that cannot be passed, then God always provides. So, will they now watch with Him, in that stillness of night when senses and susceptibilities are refined to an especial degree of knowledge? Watch: in its original Greek this word carries this sense of being awake in the night, the night which is the normal time for repose and recreation in sleep; but He begs that they shall be vigilant and stay awake. And why? Simply to be there so that He may not feel bereft of human sympathy, that He may be comforted by their presence. Stay here and watch, reports Saint Mark: stay here and watch with me, says Saint Matthew. Yet when in the unbearable restlessness of anguish Christ rises from His knees to come to them for support, even His three are asleep (worn out by grief, says Saint Luke). Why, can you not keep awake for one hour? Small wonder, though, that they shrank from seeing Jesus in this unusual condition of apparent defeat and exhaustion, He who had always been in complete command of every situation, who had never failed in control. Now He is gripped in the terror of some imminent crisis, and is failing them. Oblivion is their refuge. Once before He had begged His Father to save Him from this hour, yet, then, hardly were the words out of His mouth than He had instantly asserted that for that very hour had He come. Now it has come, the hour has struck and can it be eliminated? God is almighty, He could even now alter

SACRIFICE

the pattern of salvation and spare the beloved Son the unspeakable sufferings which are advancing fast as an engulfing tidal wave. "Father, let this hour pass." Yet not for one instant does Christ cease to struggle, cease to repudiate and resist the will, say, of His body, of His senses and emotions; He does not drop into a moment of apathy or excuse of natural weakness. All must conform to the divine will, and the energy of His deepest self, His ultimate will, must unify His whole being into choice of, not His own but the Father's will. In the abyss of His spirit He always accepts, He is ultimately obedient, yet it is on all the levels of existence that there has to be the total choice. Christ has come to the moment when suffering in its totality, in its height, breadth and depth, is offered to Him and He, with total energy, accepts it.

So intense is the tug, the strain, the conflict, that soul and body are almost rent apart and the blood which maintains His life begins to ooze through the pores of His skin. O, He must have help and relief in this intolerable anguish, seek release from the dark waters of humiliation in which He is sinking, and once more Jesus comes for it to His three closest friends. They are asleep: His loneliness is complete. Peter it is who stirs at the beloved Master's approach and hears the sad exclamation, "What, can you not watch even for one hour?" Apparently not: and Christ sees that He is to be denied all human sympathy. What a rent is made in the sacred heart as He accepts this failure of His friends' love, coupled with His knowledge that humanity will constantly, to the end of time, refuse the love with which He would serve it! For the third time Christ sinks to the ground crying aloud the same words which ring in Peter's ears, "not what I will but as Thou wilt". He continues to drink the cup of suffering from brim to dregs, as His whole soul is invaded by the sense of separation from His being, His source and end. The state of division, darkness and disintegration of body and soul which man brought upon himself by his initial act of self-enthronement, by his disobedience to the law of his created being, denying his essentially dependent nature, is now to be experienced by perfect Man who freely and of His own choice takes it upon Himself and endures what only He alone can know, the full horror and fearfulness of sin. His pure conscience is now in torment for what my clouded conscience cannot see.

When is the final sweating of a man? At his death, of which it is frequently the sign. Jesus, knowing now the reality of death, corruption and extinction as well as experiencing their cause, breaks into the great sweat of blood. Not a mild gentle perspiration but an exudation of great drops which colours the ground and stains His clothes: or how would the apostles have known? All the hate, malice and cruelties, all the antagonisms and greed of mankind, all the palpitating fear that threads through nature, all is gathered up into those drops and endured: all evil which impels us to our dreadful deeds, all our lovelessness, all is rejected in that outpouring of the life-blood of the Son of Man in His immensity of sorrow.

It is recorded that on his death-bed Charles IX of France was so conscience-stricken by the iniquity of his Saint Bartholomew's Eve massacre that his anguish of sorrow caused a bloody sweat. This fearful flow of blood will drain away the royal Lamb's life now, before He has come to the place of sacrifice, before He has obeyed to the death of the cross, and as there is no possible human help, once again a celestial creature shall succour Him. And what is the purpose of this supernatural strengthening? To maintain Jesu in life so that He may suffer yet further, and display publicly, in the face of all space and time, the whole sea of His Passion which we can never fully

SACRIFICE

fathom however often we contemplate it, however profound our response of love and thanksgiving, of veneration and contrition. Nor can we plumb the depths of Christ's zeal for the Father's honour and glory, the intensity of desire with which He participated in the Father's gift of the world's redemption; but it is here in Gethsemane that the veil is sufficiently thin for us to be able to see something of the immeasurable, incomprehensible price paid by Love. And with the soul's eye fixed upon that lonely figure, we are aware that in some degree the battle with all the forces against Him is already over, because there in the garden it has been won. With the will of His whole nature unmovably enclosed within that of the Father, Jesus now moves forward in the triumph of serenity and power to whatever sequence of suffering is ahead. He is again what the disciples have always found Him to be, the master of circumstances, the man of swift decision who moves, speaks and acts according to His own compulsion and not according to that of others. He it is who allows them their powers. This is the Jesus they know, the perfection of being, this is a glory; but it is a perfection and power which is the result of obedience to suffering. Ought not Christ to suffer and so to enter into His glory?

Not my will but Thine. Do we know what Christ means by this reiterated cry which He flings across the listening silences? Throughout His public life He has stressed the fact that He has come from heaven to earth to do not His own will but that of Him who has sent Him: that He seeks the Father's will, which is in itself actually His meat, the nourishment which sustains Him for the service of that will. When speaking of this will He more often refers to it as of 'Him who sent Me' than of 'my Father'. What had His early religious training taught Jesus about God's will, and how deeply did this concept enter into the Jewish consciousness? As we of the New Testament know it, the answer is, hardly at all, for in itself such an idea is too psychological and metaphysical to be easily acceptable to a people who were, though deeply religious, essentially objective and disinclined for the abstract. There is almost no speculation in their scriptures about the divine will, the word hardly occurs in the Old Testament, the venerated and precious Law is not displayed as God's will. But the writings which nourished our Lord are filled with conviction that God's counsels and design for the world, particularly for His chosen people, are absolute and perfect, that by His word He created all things which He maintains by His power, and that the universe reveals Him as the supreme ruler delighting in His work. He is a governor who is wholly despotic (the only form of monarchy known in the east), able to do what He pleases; and to please Him men must conform to all that He delights in. The Lord most High is essentially free to do as He chooses, it is His nature to possess the power of freedom. Communication between God and His people is a fact and reality, for His voice declares His intentions, His desires and requirements, and this voice must be obeyed. In the Old Testament, 'to hear' and 'to obey' translate the same Hebrew word, and obedience is the foundation of the relationship between the Children of Israel and their God. 'If you obey my voice I will be your God and you shall be my people.' His voice cannot contradict His nature which is transcendent in wisdom, holiness and power, and to hearken and obey is the witness of His people's filial response. Too often, all too often, reiterate the lamenting and reproachful prophets, men refuse to listen to the Almighty's voice, to accept His counsels. Our Lady Saint Mary expressed her entire conformity with God's design for her in her reply to His angelic messenger, 'be it unto me according to thy word':

words adopted by the church and used universally and daily ever since. She also said, 'behold, the Lord's slave', that is, I am pledged and bound to obedience.

Saint Mary's blessed Son went on from there. He begins with the phraseology and concepts of the Old Testament: "Blessed are they who hear the word of God and keep it", and to the tempter He says that man lives by every word which comes from the mouth of God. But, and this is noteworthy, He later declares that His food is to do the will of Him who has sent Him. In relation to Himself Jesus speaks not of doing God's word or obeying His law but of doing and fulfilling His will. This in itself is a revelation of the unique penetration and perfection of His spiritual vision and knowledge; the infallibility of Christ's religious insight and the splendour of His discernments command our homage. In His conception of the Father's will Jesus recognises and develops all the theological implications latent in the Jewish teachings on obedience to the Law and then transforms duty into an all-embracing mode of life as relationship. He reveals the necessity and the duty of obedience as being the actual reason for itself, when He raises obedience from the realm of duty to that of unitive love, for in transforming the healthful duty of obedience into a doing of the will of God, He therein discloses its reason and its ground to be in the very nature of being: and this is love. This change of view, this new emphasis, of immeasurably rich potentiality, upon God's will rather than His law, will now mould man's religious life; his whole life, for the concept of the divine will covers every aspect of existence and of man's relationship with His Creator and creation, it is therefore the ultimate foundation of all Christian conduct and devotion. The stupendous originality of this basic change may perhaps be indicated by the difference between the versions of the Lord's Prayer of

Saint Matthew and Saint Luke; not all the ancient biblical texts contain that phrase, "Thy will be done as in heaven so on earth." Our Lord's divine nature gave Him access into the farthest reaches of sublime truth. Blessed be Jesus Christ, true God and true Man.

This transformation of perception is taught by Christ more by practice than theory, embodied objectively in His own person, as it were, which is in fact His normal method of communication. He demonstrates more than He instructs, He manifests in Himself the truths we should hold, the beliefs that will shape our behaviour. Supremely does He accept and stress the law of obedience when He constantly describes His Father as 'Him that sent Me'. To be sent implies submission in the person who accepts the sending, who discharges the message or the mission. The messenger will the more completely fulfil his task as he approves and trusts the authority of the sender, as he understands his mission and can reveal and express it; the more he is at one with his superior the better will the delegate be: and this presupposes love. The Son constantly declares Himself to be in a state of complete dependence upon the Father. "The Son can do nothing of Himself, it is the Father who showeth Him all things": this is the nature of their relationship: so He is the perfect messenger and servant. Jesus will work only the Father's designs and purposes, carry out only His operations, see His creative will in all things; and this is the very reverse of personal choice, of isolated energy, of self-reliance. Over and over again He asserts that He seeks not His own will but the will of Him who sent Me, the will of my Father. Here we touch on the profound mystery of the being of the God-Man, one which transcends our understanding; yet though our intellect is dazzled by the intensity of the divine light, we can dimly conjecture how in the depths of His being the Incarnate Son sees and experiences the absolute will which is the sole ground of His own will. Into the Father's will the Son pours, instant by instant, the determination of His choice, as concomitantly He opens, with all the energy of His being, His faculties to perceive and receive the divine will. There is never an impulse of self away from the supreme will, never a deviation. This is because of the union of the Persons, in the Incarnate Lord, which yet contains the two natures, human and divine, each with its will which operates only in respect of that to which it pertains. The Son's human will, which operated by grace in a fullness beyond anything we can approach, is fully and perfectly in subjection to the divine will; and it derives its glorious freedom from this dependence. Here we adore.

Yet alongside this complete dependence of the Son upon the Father, the Gospels display Our Lord Christ as a man cast in a heroic mould of amazing assurance, self-assurance if you like; one who claims for Himself total allegiance, unqualified acceptance, complete knowledge of all truth, one who dazzled, commanded, awed, and yet was worshipped by His fellowmen. None before or since has claimed what Jesus claims: "the Father works, I work"; none has said without qualification, demanding acceptance, "I say unto you". He proclaims Himself as infallible. But these seemingly incompatible states, of complete dependence on and obedience to the Father's will and of unparalleled and boundless authority concentrated in His own person, are reconciled in the condition which He alone could declare: "I and the Father are one." He is what He is because the Father wills it, and He is Himself because He expresses that will in perfect obedience. Only the immensity of the Incarnation can contain all paradoxes, the only key is the union of two natures in one Person: Jesus Christ is God, is Man. O that we would all, priests and people alike, give ourselves to the work, arduous and costly as it may be, of regular, persevering, deep meditation upon Jesus Christ our Lord: and this in no external fashion, because such a Person is a unique and fascinating study, but because it is the only way to know Him, and to know is to wonder and admire, it is to exult and glory in Him, it is to love; and through the exercise of all our faculties and sentiments we then learn to find and use Him as our life. Let us each come to the vision of Christ as best we may, by the eyes of the mind or by the eyes of the heart, for it alone reveals the meaning of life.

And it was there in the garden of Gethsemane that Christ for our sakes revealed in Himself the stark naked struggle of humanity to maintain obedience to the divine will, which alone is its freedom, its necessity, its glory. "Not my will but Thine": the choice of the triumphant suffering servant of Glory. Yet He has never posed our human query, why? But the moment is at hand when Jesus on the cross, torn, shredded, in the embrace of foul dereliction, asks why? Invaded by evil, bearing all sin, when His humanity is confronted with obliteration, with extinction, He cries, 'why?' All is thick blackness, the understanding can receive no answer. The unbearable moment is upon Him, that moment which He accepts in Gethsemane, and He bears it because faith lives, hope persists, love prevails, so that even before the question is asked answer is affirmed: "My God, my God." My Jesus, perfect man, endures through the unendurable to which He has given Himself, until at long last all is complete, fulfilled, consummated. The work He has been sent to do is obediently done, and in peace He offers all. "Father, into thy hands I commend my spirit." God is again Father. The Son through obedience to the will of infinite Life has experienced and overcome that which would annihilate it in dissolution of life, and He knows again the light of the divine relationship. And relationship reminds us that throughout the agony of the cross to the final moment of literal heart-break, our Lady, His mother and ours, stands beside Him. Can we doubt that in the mighty strength of her pure love she not only supported her Son but in desire and simplicity of will sped Him onwards to His consummation; that her pure vision saw the beauty of His soul in sacrifice, saw the real glory of its suffering?

For in that suffering and death was wrought a transmutation of the concept of sacrifice. By a stupendous act of interiorisation, sacrifice was translated from the sphere of exterior action to that of spiritual activity; an act which the Son of God alone could make and present to man for his acceptance and practice. External rites of sacrifice, rich in meaning and symbolism, holy and fervent in function, which have for so long been the method of worship and service of a righteous God, earth's creator and king, are now to be finalised in an interior, spiritual offering of a man's whole being, an offering which consists of the acceptance and deliberate use of suffering and death. In this one particular hour of time the intrinsic act of sacrifice is lifted out of the sphere of objective matter into the inner core of man's self, it is changed from a process which demands external material, conditions and ritual to a simple unity of interior action involving the purest operation of spirit. Never has there been such an overwhelming act of interiorisation. In Christ's experience sacrifice has become passive as regards infliction, passive as is the lamb led to the slaughter, but wholly active in respect of the will which presents the offering; and thus the offerer and the offered, priest and victim, subject and object, are, for the first time in history, effectively one. In the depths of His being, with an overwhelming single intensity of concentration of every faculty and power, Christ gives, to receive—nothing. This is the consummation of sacrifice. The rolling centuries of holocausts have led up to this unique moment which both justifies and fulfils them, and never more shall they have reason or necessity. We are held in awed wonder at the sublime majesty of this unique divine sacrifice, which alone leads man into a worship of God which is in spirit and truth. It is no surprise, though it is a miracle, that at this moment the immense veil in the Temple is split, for there is now a newness of vision and of worship beyond all foretelling and foreseeing. There will be no more altars of sacrifice, only the one altar of the cross.

But man is now ready for the spiritual worship at that altar only through his gradual assimilation of the reality and necessity of sacrifice which has been relayed to him through his long historical apprenticeship to the function of offering material and physical things, bodies and blood. "Behold, the Lamb of God!" That is how the last and greatest of the prophets acclaimed his cousin Jesus, for John the Baptist saw with an amazing clarity of spiritual insight that the Man standing there by the river's bank was the antetype of all the lambs sacrificed on Jewish altars; and every Jew who heard that phrase would understand its meaning and could remark its inference, that this man Jesus was sealed for sacrifice. But without its Old Testament background John's statement is meaningless. The features and practice of a religion of altar, priesthood and sacrifice, allied to a monotheistic faith itself essentially noble and elevating, is the priceless heritage of every Jew, having an incalculable power to satisfy and deepen all yearnings for God, for personal consecration and holiness. Even though the rites and sacrifices were but shadows and types of reality, God's mercy blessed them to His worshippers, and the Holy Spirit, whose movement initiated them, employed them to awaken and inform men's perceptions concerning the final Reality who would in His own Person reveal their meaning. How impressive is the magnitude and intricacy of this vast tapestry of religious sacrifice spread across those centuries when God's chosen people were slowly and painfully working out their national vocation, and how we are exalted as we ponder over the sublime design! The sensitive imagination dilates. Painters, such as Jan Van Eyck, have been captured by the excitement of the subject and tried nobly to portray it, but it is almost beyond realisation in the sphere of the visible and sensible. The mind can float only so far on the waters of visual art, then it must take wing and soar aloft in the intangible air of thought, even beyond words. To go as far as we can intellectually in examination of this spiritual evolution of the concept of sacrifice brings us inevitably to the manifestation of the Word-made-flesh, who is the beginning and end of all truth for us in this world. And something more than the exercise of the intellect is required to perceive that here on the cross which held the Lamb of God the rite of sacrifice is charged with a new, a unique energy of power: an energy which itself could have burst open the heart of the victim, whose life was terminated not by physical collapse but by the intensity of His creative offering of His whole being, the offering of Man to God by God.

Standing now before the cross, gazing at the crucified Lord, we cannot fail to recognise the centrality of His whole life and purpose of this His offering of Himself, the total renunciation in the unity of body, soul and spirit, in obedience to suffering and death. To acknowledge it as His destiny is to accept it in some sense as ours also: we are involved but whether as one on the far edge of the crowd or as one close to the Cross, whether as one blind or seeing, refusing or adoring, mocking or grieving, ah, there is the choice. For it is not possible to isolate Christ's

Passion from the germination of earth's first seed or the birth of the latest baby, from the sunrise or the squall, from love's intercourse or hate's murder, any more than you can dissever a feature from a face and still claim to know the whole physiognomy. It is as clear as desert air that the crucifixion is integral to creation and therefore, most mysteriously to God Himself, since God ineffably willed to create and there can be no division in the eternal will of Godhead. The divine operations visible to us in time and space are one mighty whole conceived in unity, they are the Word once spoken which forever speaks, they are one immensity of dramatic harmony which in its grandeur, majesty, glory is beyond our grasp but within our adoration, praise, humility. As far as this world is concerned, this divine drama does not arrive at a static end with the death of Incarnate God, not even with the ineluctable sequel of resurrection and ascension. For that freely-willed obedience on cavalry of the Son of Man to His Father is a universal offering made not only for us but one in which we all need to be found, to have our place. That perfect and glorious Manhood, which encompasses all humanity as far as humanity will accept it, is the instrument of loving sacrifice unto death whereby its offerer compensates for the sin of all mankind and restores it potentially to its participation in the divine life. But Jesus does not ask us to consider this intellectually, to look at the mystery from outside, we are enjoined to enter into His action.

In effect, our Lord says, Here am I, actually and really, though in a new mode, so take Me into yourself that you may realise that I take you and offer you with Myself in my atoning sacrifice: do not merely remember what once and for all time I have done for you, but do something, which will make your remembering immeasurably more interior, more penetrating, more vital. It is by an activity provided by God that we enter into an assured climax of relationship with the Holy Trinity, a climax which gives the soul a place and a moment for concentrated adoration, thanksgiving, penitence and love. The communication of the reality of Christ's sacrifice to each individual is visibly displayed in the eucharistic dispensation of His Body and Blood, to endure to the end of time. For this end Christ formed His church, to be the guardian and the channel of God's final creative operations, the outpouring of grace by the Holy Spirit in the sacraments. Convolutions of blessing, of supernature working in nature, of the life of the spirit, here baffle us by their complexity and their wonder; but they all revolve upon the mystery of the unity of suffering and glory. 'Dying, behold we live', we really do.

> *O most sweet memorial of Thy death and woe,*
> *Living bread which givest life to men below,*
> *Let my spirit ever eat of Thee and live*
> *And the blest fruition of Thy sweetness give.*

In what surer, safer manner could the knowledge of the essential, saving act of divine love be preserved for all time, available for all men, than by the rite of the Eucharist? Action would guarantee more than words, therefore, 'this do in remembrance', was His revelation, His design, together with His own declaration of what 'this' is. And because of the 'this', the doing will be not only a presentation of theological doctrine and food for men's minds, it will also be the real presence able to stir and enliven the spiritual faculties as powerfully as any appearance of the resurrected Lord to disciples in Galilee. No reading of holy scripture can so serve, for although the word of God is a living thing declaring and revealing to us both the Lord and the way of life, it cannot actually give us that Life. In the supreme sacrament of the Body of Christ He communicates to us the virtue of His perfect humanity, in which He is forever offering worship to the Godhead, communicates the power to participate in the love in which He eternally dwells, and lifts us into the immensity of His heart's desire for the joy and fulfilment of all creation. Taking us into Himself, according to our purity and power to give ourselves to Him, He makes us one offering with Himself. This great mystery is the heart, the centre, the fountain of all Christian worship; this it has been from the first days of the church, this it ever will be, despite all the changes and chances of error which inevitably have beset it, as Christianity's developing mind has tried, and that rightly, to explore all its meanings and implications, its values and practical usage. Marvellous and gracious is the act of communion but it is not the sole purpose of the Eucharist; the response, quality and range of Christian worship, and of individual devotion both private and public, will suffer if the emphasis placed on that aspect of the rite diminishes attention to the essential element of its sacrifice, an element which in regard to the worshipper is both commemorative and unitive. Whenever we are present at this service, whether we communicate or not, we concentrate all the powers of the soul on the whole oblation of His life which Jesus made to the Father in His death, and in union with Him we plead it for the needs, especial and general, of the whole world. Having with us at our altar the presence of the Lord of the resurrection, alive for evermore, we know that He is pleading His sacrifice in the heavenlies even as we are representing it on earth. And all our personal sacrifices, offerings, sufferings, are united with His and taken by Him into the cup of His offerings, the offering which contains every element of relationship. It is a valuable spiritual exercise, devout and enlarging, sometimes to be present at the Eucharist without communicating, when we may concentrate objectively on the aspects of thanksgiving, intercession, contrition; this will help us to maintain some proportion between its two supreme functions. For this our bounden duty and service is of such majestic range, has such a truly godlike fulfilment, that human limitations do not allow us to use immensely all its possibilities at one time. But whatever we do, it is a doing of divine appointment, this glad and glorious sacrament of sacrifice and unity which makes us one with our God and one with each other.

"You must sit down," says Love, "and taste my meat,"
So I did sit and eat.

Love ties us in the knot of obedience.

DETACHMENT

Having nothing yet possessing all things.

We have traced in the words and actions of the Lord Christ a sequence of logical developments relating to suffering, obedience, will and sacrifice; have we established the relevance of our own sufferings? For it is my own troubles which matter to me, which must be handled and lived with, which can make life almost intolerable with a past so heavy and a future unpromisingly grey. Where lies the practical relationship between Christ's afflictions and mine? What am I to do? To raise and harden the voice on that last question is legitimate, for life is not lived without doing, and action demands thought, choice and will, all personal to me.

How inexorable is the passing of time! Persistent, relentless, inflexible, the minutes come, the minutes go, days follow days, time's division succeeds division and nothing in life can halt the march. This is a fascinating thought. Though I myself become unconscious and lie in a coma I am carried along on a stream of succession; when I recover I find myself many hours forward from the point when I ceased to know time by the clock or by the shadows. I choose and determine so much of my activity and circumstance, particularly am I very much in control of trivial occurrences and general business, so that up to a point my personal decisions order what shall fill the hours;

DETACHMENT

but I cannot order the hours, which can never be shortened or prolonged or obliterated. "Time doesn't exist," said the young man in the café, loudly, "it doesn't exist, we have created it." The girl who was with him was not intelligent. Have we indeed? We create the measurement, but we live in time from which there is no escape: we have not made it and cannot break it. What does not exist can be ignored, but we cannot ignore time. There is witness to this in the fairy- and folk-tales which relate the sudden disappearance of a man from his place into some other dimension of time. When he returns to his home years, even centuries later, he may be of the same age as he was at his departure, but he is to discover that his contemporaries are now aged beyond recognition, or are many years dead, and he himself is known only as a memory. Time is as real as our dimensional life in space and accompanies it beyond our manipulation. In fact in these remarkable days of technology man does much to alter space by reducing hills, filling up seas, diverting rivers, and so on, but he cannot get rid of an instant of time. 'Time is a thing that no man may resist.' Until the end of time it issues forth from eternity, and God is its creator, as much the Lord of seconds as of aeons, holding all within His absolute will.

It follows then that time must be of unique importance, for nothing which depends unconditionally upon the divine will can be otherwise than of infinite value, conditional and finite though it may be in itself. It is within this flow of succession, this ceaseless sweep of change and limit, that God operates that which shall best avail His creatures for their highest good, that is, what shall most freely advance their union with Himself, their glory. In simplest terms, that which occurs to me outwardly at any one moment is for my good and is the best means, once it has happened, of drawing me towards holiness, for God's will has allowed it; whether by permission or immediately it is not possible or necessary here to discuss. The certainty is, that it is the divine action which influences each moment and so provides me with the circumstances in which I can love Him and love my neighbour, the two loves being inseparable. This does not, of course, imply mechanical conditioning, for no events are independent of human wills which, though limited and relative, are free and personal forces which produce contingent effects. Circumstances and experiences not of my primary choice or particular wish are forced upon me; they may, indeed, be the very reverse of desirable, they may be conducive of discomfort, a maze of hurtful contradiction, but as God is almighty they cannot thwart His purpose for me, which is my blessedness and sure safety in the spirit. Nothing can obstruct the fullness of His love. True, by the culpable failure of my will to goodness I may fill any moment with deed or thought which is dark, evil, in which I, so to speak, turn my back on light and refuse to allow His will to be done by me; but I cannot refuse His power, for moment by moment I receive from Him the freedom to accept or decline His light and His law. Even my sin cannot remove me from the will of God, which in the very moment that I have misused operates towards me both in justice and in mercy.

There is great and lovely simplicity in this exercise, one day to become habitual, of seeing and receiving the present moment and all that it contains as a sacramental which conveys through the outward and external happening the inward spiritual thing which is not more nor less than the will of the Father. 'Each minute taken separately is the dear will and direct vehicle of God,' said Baron von Hügel. And does it make any difference to my practice if the moments are those of unhappiness and pain? Of course not. I take them as what He allows me, and that cannot be apart from His wisdom and graciousness; and, I am prompted to do this confidently because I have studied the pains of Jesus Christ and filled my memory with an intimate knowledge of the exemplar of all suffering. Apart from Him, I should not know what to do with the illnesses and the fears, the tempers, trials and bitter misunderstandings from which none is immune, I should have no authority to justify my attitude. But from Jesus, and from Him only, I have learnt to accept. I assent to the moment because God allows it to me, I dissent from any temptation, sin, evil and defect which it may present. Get thee behind me, Satan! Both movements are possible in one rhythm and both may be required, even as breathing-in and breathing-out constitute one whole act. Faced with its pain, a man may too easily dissent from the whole moment in its entirety, not discerning the Lord's body, which is His will within. Suffering, time, the will of God: let us admit that some people find this a faulty solution to their problem. "Suffering," writes the author of the newspaper's religious column, "should not be described as sent." But may we say, rather, 'provided', for we have already acknowledged that without the provision of suffering we should have no salvation, seeing that Jesus, the author of eternal salvation, accomplished it for us through the things which He suffered. Of course it must depend, as the writer rather querulously comments, on the individual's attitude as to whether suffering purifies, as the clergy teach, or whether it embitters; but is this more surprising or regrettable than that, say, our attitude to wine may leave us either refreshed or drunk, that upon our attitude to highway traffic depends our safety? Attitude is necessary to everything; but what a little is required! Those who seem to be spoiled by suffering could well be much more spoiled without it. And one receives so many illustrations of the truth that the poverty of pain does convey blessing when it is accepted; in manners, in refinement of mind and sensitivity, the incurable invalid may be greatly superior to the rest of the family. How often we observe, humbly and thankfully, a man's growth in nobility and integrity against the background of unusual blows: blows of fate says the world, of providence says the Christian.

There are several fruitful and abiding dispositions which are necessary as we adjust ourselves to all forms of suffering, they open out of and depend upon each other. It is faith in God, and faith alone, which enables me to receive and assent to His adorable will in the encounters of each moment. Everything always begins with faith and returns to it, the blessed gift of faith which is ours by virtue of baptism, the foundation of all our life of grace in Christ. Who shall sing the song of faith? It is no cool act of the intellect, no easy shrug of assent, no thoughtless or superficial impulse, though any of these could contain its potentiality. Faith grows and deepens according to the soul's religious development, from a simple act of belief in God and His word with which a child begins to a movement of the entire being towards God and in God, involving mind, heart and will; more than a movement, it becomes a state from which it is impossible to remove, a state which maintains the soul in that union with God which His love grants it. Through the practice of prayer it gains increasing facility in gathering together all the interior powers into a unity directed towards God: this is faith, this is what our Lord requires of us when He asks, 'do you now believe?' Because in this life our unity is never total, our giving is never whole and entire, so even when we reply, 'yes Lord, I believe,' we add: 'help thou my unbelief.'

The growth of faith depends not upon reaching out to an

exterior force but upon our co-operation with a virtue which we already possess through grace, therefore by the strength, intensity and perseverance of our specific acts of faith made in prayer both public and private, vocal and by less formal aspiration. Never do we outgrow acts of faith, which can be either the prelude to interior prayer or the entire state; and if in times of dryness our initial act of faith is no more than a struggle to assent to the Lord of life, our persistence can transform it into a way of union, dark rather than light. But we have literally to act, to live our faith, not merely say it, and it will deepen according to the measure of trust which we give God in the circumstances of life. Just as we try to acquire any necessary virtue by moral force and actual practice, compelling ourselves if, for instance, we are establishing the virtue of gentleness, to speak and move gently, to scrutinise our courtesies and restraints, so it is by deliberate exercise that we build up the habit of faith. It will not grow by itself apart from our efforts. Faith grows when tested by opposition, when proved by what seems impossible, therefore trials have a definite value in relation to it. And, in the reverse direction, what actually does faith provide relative to trials of any sort whatsoever? Simply the conviction that all shall be well, that all is well, for God holds all: so, blessed be God. Whether struggle, resistance and holy combat are required or whether the attitude must be submission and meekness, whether there is grief or glee, light or gloom, the soul strong in faith accepts whatever the moment provides believing that it holds and unfolds the purpose of God. He wills our glory and joy, Christ assures us, for our glory is His, His ours, and every circumstance ministers to it in so far as we accept and obey His will.

Long before the Light of the world declared faith to be the

foundation of salvation the Jews of the Old Covenant had affirmed it and responded to it grandly. Could any call to trust be plainer than Isaiah's message from God given in words warm in the divine love and promise (43, 1–3):

> Fear not: for I have redeemed thee,
> I have called thee by My name;
>   Thou art mine.
> When thou passeth through the waters I will be with thee.

Who could fail to respond with faith? Jesus our Lord lived by it. But we err if we suppose that, because it is essentially required of us, faith is an easy matter, and that a person who is without it is voluntarily walking in the dark without regret for the light. To leap a chasm between what may be likely and what appears impossible may at a particular time and place be beyond an unbeliever's moral honesty and volition. He may be so conditioned by and attached to his reflective processes that he cannot reach out in blind faith to pass beyond ratiocination in this one act of assent to something which appears to surpass, though it never denies, the grasp of the intellect. Faith asks for self-detachment. We also err if we think that we are so firmly established that we can never lose it or suffer any diminishment. What we took for granted as an unassailable position may be attacked, what we assumed as firm ground may slip beneath our feet, darkness can invade any soul however mature, and temptations assault it all unexpectedly. In temporal life there is no once-and-for-all certainty even in the spiritual life: there is a recurring sign by the wayside, 'take heed lest ye fall.' So Jesus said, and so I cry, Lord, increase my faith, ever increase it and maintain it within the security of my union with yourself. Faith demands humility and great simplicity.

DETACHMENT

I am the child of God,
I ought to do His will,
I can do what He tells me to,
And by His grace I will.

The most profound truths are sometimes simplest said. "Except you become as little children you cannot enter the kingdom." But there is nothing childish in that faith which sustains a soul in its loving adherence to God even in the hour of its Gethsemane, in the hour of its crucifixion: it then needs all the strength of maturity.

It is by faith that I try to accept all that seems to thwart and ill-use me, physically and materially, all that the world calls misfortunes, for I believe that they are the means provided by God for deepening my life in Christ: the only life which will endure into eternity when death destroys my earthly place. By faith I believe that only through the trials which God allows shall I learn certain realities of the spiritual life: irrespective of the sort of trials, for from experience I learn how valuable physical suffering and illness can be in regard to these realities. Faith it is which enables me to accept and use any type of trouble, with both hands if I can, as, in its moment, my immediate way of union with God, for if suffering is indeed part of the answer to the lock of life, then faith is the first key to use.

Let us acknowledge that any condition of suffering may be much more difficult to accept when it is imposed not directly upon ourselves but on someone whom we know, with whom we are allied, whom we dearly love. 'God can't be good if He allows this,' is a common expression of rebellion framed when tragedy wounds a friend, and it can prove to be a first step on the road to refusal of God. But God has to be accepted whole, for He either is, or is not: if He is, then His almighty will cannot be anything else but good and all that He allows is good: blessed may He be. God is love, and could be no God unless He were exactly this; it follows that He cannot act against love, range Himself opposite to it. Our acceptance of whatever the moment holds has to be made for others equally as for ourselves, even though our compassion, or our struggle against evil, rightly impels us to do all in our power to alleviate and remove their sorrows. The energy of our faith may be required to communicate a radiance to support them in their need.

How often Jesus cried, "I know": "I know my Father"; for His faith was knowledge. He alone is our way to the Father, He is the giver of that faith which carries us, as Saint Paul said, into His Bosom, and perhaps when we have given ourselves to Him in an ardour of self-detachment and generosity, we also shall be so saturated with faith that we can humbly say, 'we know.' By divine enlightenment, and by ways of self-denial and prayer, belief in the things of God may be so strong as to be almost sight; but it all rests upon the basic lesson of discipleship which must be strenuously upheld, that whatever the moment holds is (my deliberate choice of sin excepted) the shortest way for me to God and my essential peace. So it is that my faith directs me to accept and use whatever trials and tribulations are my lot: but 'use' covers a wide field of activity.

Our Lord reveals His intensity of faith in His unbounded confidence in His Father's power, His unhesitating assumption of infallibility and authority which depended for its sole source on the Father's will. It was this trust and confidence which urged Him forward to the obedience of sacrifice which His ardent love burned to offer. "I have a baptism to be baptised

DETACHMENT

with: how intensely I long for its accomplishment, its consummation." So must it be with us. From our faith in God's will springs our confidence that we shall have grace to fulfil it, a confidence which helps us to overcome the hardships and humiliations, often so unfathomable and surprising, which life presents. There is no arrogance or self-sufficiency in holy confidence, it is stayed upon humility. I am nothing of myself, in my own power and strength I do nothing of value but I can do and bear the impossible through Christ and His grace. The more I can see and acknowledge my nothingness (and this whatever the talents and gifts with which God has endowed me) the deeper is my rest upon God, my dependence upon Him for grace, my full abandonment to His will and my pliability in circumstances, in all of which is peace, is hope and joy. It was our Lord's way. "The Son can do nothing of Himself but what He sees the Father doing" . . . "nothing of myself but as the Father taught me." The communion of Jesus with His Father throbs with passionate confidence. Yet I may have no consciousness of trust as I carry my heavy burden, all my energies, both interior and external, may be absorbed in struggling to accept it uncomplainingly and willingly, as were Christ's in the agony in the garden; but if faith is authentic and vital it is accompanied by the activity of confidence without any feeling of it, as certainly as wetness accompanies water. So I am held in inner calm and spiritual strength, a calm which can astonish me when it is maintained in the face of tempests of evil and wickedness and persecution.

Further, just because I have a living relationship with Almighty God whose will I adore, I am bound to receive my sufferings with deliberate thankfulness. How can I do otherwise, when I have agreed that everything He allows is for my good and glory, because all proceeds ultimately from the mystery of love which is Himself? Though the trial seems intolerable and is straining me to my limits of endurance, I can make it at once both more acceptable and more readily sustained when, relaxing into it with my will's compliance, I bless God, I force myself to give thanks. It is not only for this and that satisfaction, beauty and good that I have received, not only for the richnesses woven into my life, not only for the laughter but also for the tears, for this very anguish, this sacramental moment heavy with woe, that I bless Him. My thanking is within every moment without exception. I am not trying to escape from it, O my God, I am trying to take hold of it and use it as a sacrifice and an offering of love, for what else have I at this moment to give You? This is what my suffering is for, so, all praise and thanks, my Father. "I will sing of the Lord because He is dealing so lovingly with me." I have no feeling of this now, but when the dark pain has passed, or at least lessened, I realise that, not according to this world's standards, but in the deep places of the spirit, God has indeed dealt lovingly with me, for He knows me and my needs; and my determination to sing of Him, even though I am out of tune, has lifted me above the temporal entanglement with the misery and helped to prevent me from centring myself in it, particularly in respect of my emotions. Thanksgiving strangles self-pity. Easily we give natural thanks for any kindness, for delights, but giving it supernaturally for hurt and pain produces a great richness of heart which uncovers the truth that in accepting God's will we do indeed choose our sure happiness. Experience is gained by a progress of circles.

Yet how absurd it must seem to the world, how impossible, for me to thank any God for the bitter woe in which I am almost drowning, for the excruciating pain against which my heart cries out that it need not have been if . . . if only: there is

DETACHMENT

always an 'if'. "O no!" is the immediate cry flung upon the shrinking air: "O no!" answered Peter when he received the Lord's warning of His coming passion and cruel death: "O no!" is inevitably man's response to the sight of the sword which brings the expulsion from paradise. Yet that negation's reverse is not only "O yes!" but also, "God, I bless you", even though the time of wrestling be a long one. We ourselves may not have the patriarch Jacob's sense of seeing God in the struggle but after it is over we know that, as at Peniel, God has indeed given His blessing through it. What seems absurd, unreasonable, makes sense in the end if the end be God. The outward movement of thankfulness itself enlarges the soul beyond the self which Jesus said must be denied.

We know only too well that it is possible for a person to turn in upon himself and lose significance under the pressure of physical infirmity and difficult circumstances, appearing to diminish in reality until his emptiness becomes almost tangible. From such a person complaint, peevishness, mean grumbling, scorn of others, trickles like a continual upthrow of dirty water from a blocked pipe. Such a person may actually be quite brave in bearing bodily pain, but it is a hard, self-contained fortitude, useful in defending the ego from others' pity and giving it prestige in its own eyes, obscuring the sight and knowledge of the individual's real selfishness and limitations. Contrariwise, although an old woman who in a similar situation, with diminishing mental powers and failing limbs, may seem at a casual encounter also to be very empty, a deeper and more perceptive reception will prove that she actually conveys an impression of fulfilment and blessedness: she possesses the reality of otherworldly values. Her interest does not centre on herself; all unconsciously she has achieved an abiding place of self-detachment, and there is beauty. Achieved is probably the right word to use. Such a one may never have consciously practised detachment by careful prescription of rules of self-denial, she may indeed have only a most elementary understanding of devotion *per se*, but simply as a faithful servant of God she has all her life, all unawares, made use of its trials, the lesser equally with the great. They have been accepted without bitterness, recrimination or loss of love, and so they have worn away the self's concern for its own wishes and interests, until the self for self's sake is hardly there. In the ordinariness of life her cross has done its work and the result is glory. There is a radiance about such a simple person, which is not surprising for she has, according to the light given, lived the beatitudes and, "blessed are the poor", whether in goods or in spirit. Patience is often their only medicine, their only cure: it is the rich who can go hither and thither trying this and then that remedy and diversion, sometimes augmenting the ills and conditions they deplore by their interest in the many avenues of treatment available for their minds and bodies. The poor and the meek can only abide in patience; and as patience itself is a sharing of the sufferings of Christ, they have their reward. The Christ cannot make false promises.

Why are our pastors afraid to press upon us continually and urgently the basic condition of all Christian life: "If any man will be My disciple, let him deny himself daily, take up his cross and follow Me." No necessity could be plainer. And although we may go as far as desire impels in the personal choice of ways of self-denial and be very resolute in self-discipline, it is life itself with the duties and responsibilities, with the crises, perplexities and tensions that are imposed on all of us as we accept relationship, which provide the denying and the cross; and also the road of love, for nothing can be done apart from love. But this acceptance of life is not what the self wants.

DETACHMENT

Because of the twist in human nature, its desires are towards itself and its personal satisfactions so that it seeks what it selects as its good, it manipulates circumstances to its own end, hiding from the Light which would show it something different. Today's growth of psychological explanations of behaviour provides us with a store of fascinating and successful excuses, such as inherited characteristics, juvenile inhibitions, buried fears, assumed ignorances and, above all, frustrations: what should we do without our private frustrations! Yet explain it as you will, this is the mystery in which we are involved, this crookedness of being which prevents us from seeing where our true happiness lies and from pursuing it at all costs: though men seldom doubt that they are made for happiness. This belief is in fact confirmed to us by Christ, for He said that His kingdom is happiness, is leaping for joy, and that although it is heaven and eternal it begins now, within the soul, in the depths of present being. He came to reveal and call me to enter into this joy, with one declared condition of participation, namely the loosening of self in ever-deepening degrees from all that seems to constitute what I think of as myself and my claims. Everything that keeps my senses clinging to and feeding upon their pleasures, anything which encourages me to assert that I cannot live without it, any chain which ties me into knots of self-love, all this I must cut, pluck out, break, or beg God to do so for me. People and occasions, pursuits and pleasures, none bad in themselves, can any of them hinder not only my whole-hearted love of God by entangling me in themselves, but also my real love of man, therefore they call for denial. I am split into a hundred selves as I run after this and that with insistence and clamour; God, however, intends me as a unity, as one energy of being without division, which shall be directed wholly towards Himself the All containing all, the supreme source of

Glory, perfection of Bliss, He who alone can fulfil and satisfy. To arrive at such a unity I must be empty of all self-motivation, self-stirrings, self-absorption: what else is Our Lord saying with His 'deny'? And as I find myself in Him because He fills more and more of me, I shall receive back double, treble, a hundred fold, of whatever I have given up for His sake; I receive it literally, in my powers of discernment, appreciation, fulfilment, in sheer happiness, in enlargement of soul. If the riches, the worth, the wisdom of detachment are proved by experience to be the source of pure joy, its process cannot be deplored or refused by him who chooses joy, any more than is the decomposition of the seed when it has generated that new plant which is its glory.

> *Mine heart, my mind, my thought, my whole delight*
> *Is, after this life, to see Thy glorious face.*

But the seeing, even though it is in a dim mirror, begins in this life and therefore so does the delight. This day is salvation come, this day is glory.

So, by grace I welcome whatever suffering the moments bring to me, simply because it will do so much of my work for me: it is as when the rain saves me the labour of watering my flower-beds by hand. Just so far as I can make spiritual use of my trials, even of my mistakes and deficiencies, will they avail for purifying my motives and intentions, will they rub away some of the rust of my faults as surely as oil loosens the cog-wheel; in fact, rather than making use of them, I might say that they use me. Pain uses me because as my energies are directed towards bearing it with these necessary dispositions of faith, humility, thankfulness and detachment, they are not available for my monotonous self-assurance and self-pity. I can all too easily enjoy and gratify myself in the warmth of health,

DETACHMENT

wealth and success, even enjoy their opportunities for beneficence and bounty, which can spring from self-love rather than pure kindliness and compassion. But in the impotence of suffering and of failure there is no pedestal for pride; I have nothing to give, I can only receive, humbly dependent upon the goodwill of others. This meek acceptance of adversity, the opposite of a pretended indifference or proud resignation, not only smooths the way of suffering but gives it an eternal value, which is what stoicism cannot do. Surely we can see the simplicity of line in this divine economy which administers suffering as a means of purification. O blessed suffering, whose gifts include a mirror in which I can see myself for what I really am, which discloses truth, even as in winter the denuded trees and hedges reveal the naked buildings, back-yards and derelict patches normally screened by leafage. All God's faithful children testify that it is through their sorrows and griefs they have learnt of the realities of the spirit and received deep insights into the ways of union with Christ rather than in the years of comfort and ease. "In no other way could I have learnt what I now know", is the common cry. The grey doors of time begin already to glow with the gold of eternity when the light falls on the right place.

As we explore the life and character of Jesus Christ we are compelled to acknowledge His regal freedom of soul, the ease and grandeur with which He possesses Himself. Time does not seem to restrict or constrain Him for He does not use it for Himself but for people, to whom He is always wholly accessible. He goes out of His way to respond to appeals for help, He accepts, and commands, all sorts of hospitality, turns aside at the touch of a woman, remains for hours, even days, where the crowds have gathered to listen to Him. Wherever He is Jesus is at men's disposal, sometimes only the night remains to Him for uninterrupted accessibility to His Father who is always accessible to Him. He seems to dominate time by His sure knowledge of the precise moment for His activities, unerring in His decisions when to remain in seclusion, when to go up to Jerusalem; He knows the time which requires Him and which He requires for the culmination of His work. He never moved too slowly, He never ran too fast. Constantly He reveals His heroic stature by the manner in which He shapes all that time and space offer; and He supplies the reason for His unfaltering judgements. "I do nothing of Myself, I do always what pleases my Father." Thus He shines the torch on His secret, which is His complete detachment from self as the guide and mainspring of personality. Such a condition of adherence to which Jesus so frequently refers is only possible through His renunciation of the operations of His ego, which He accepts as the instrument but not the source of His powers: He can do no less than require the same condition for His friends. "Deny yourself": and no one is exempt, the gospel being universal; though the range of detachment will vary with the depths of inwardness to which souls are called and respond.

She was rich, she had every comfort of home and service and her family and responsibilities required her to maintain the social position her wealth sustained. Life seemed to give her everything and demand little. How, she asked, could she practise self-denial and detachment? The Lord Christ knew that to have possessions of any sort is a challenge to the Christian to sit lightly to them, to live within their comfort without insisting on their necessity and to use them as channels of service to the brethren. Even luxury can be defeated by simplicity, and still more by joy. It is right to rejoice in the beauty, the skill and the good craftsmanship of things in our environment, be they few or many. It is only when we enjoy

DETACHMENT

them possessively as personal property which confers power, when we appraise their crude worth instead of their intrinsic beauty, when we use them to enhance our superiority, that they must become a wall between us and God from whom is all beauty. The values of truth, beauty and goodness can exist in a stewpan as well as in a Ming vase: different in degree, granted, but each a possible source of rejoicing which opens us to divine life. For to rejoice objectively in any value wherever it is displayed should ultimately lead us to delight in its Source, finally we may rejoice immediately in God and realise the thing's glory only within Him. That is the true blessedness reached when detachment is so complete that it is answered by fulfilment, as the Lord promised; for though He said that riches were a difficulty, He also said that with God nothing is impossible. It is not necessary to be a rich young ruler to sin by excessive attachment, anyone can be possessed by their dependence upon their chosen habits of certain foods, by their insistence on their whimsies, by clinging to a few useless possessions. What is it that, apart from reasonable necessities, I insist on having or upon doing, what annoys and irritates me, what deprivations upset my tranquillity? The answers will indicate where my renunciations must lie, which will be either by total refusals or by occasional omissions, according to love; and always both taste and desire will be loosened when the soul turns in thanksgiving to God. The act of blessing God impels us to wait upon Him instead of upon our selves, any glad acknowledgement of His bounty lifts us above all immoderation. Blessed be Thou in this lovely thing!

What a mercy that the church has given us rules of fasting and an ordered Lent which implant the principle of denying the body as well as the soul. "I don't think anything of your church fasting," he said to me, "simply lessening your intake and this paltry no meat once a week. When I go for one of my cures I have to abstain from all solid food for days." Very likely, but it is the motive which matters in the kingdom of God. A nature-cure fast or a slimming diet is undertaken for natural (and perhaps good) reasons, to restore damaged health and vitality, whereas a religious fast, even of small dimensions, is an offering to God of a sign of penitence and of willingness to live not only according to nature (as we must) but also by grace (as we should). Fasting is a reminder that self-denial is accepted and practised only because it is Christ's condition of discipleship, so that we may grow in the power to say with Saint Paul, 'not I but Christ'; not I: this is an obedience of love. Not the extent of the fast but the pulse of the heart which prompts it is what makes the sacrifice acceptable in heaven.

A practice of detachment which is essential for us all is self-examination to show us our faults and defects, which we cannot hate and try to remove unless we know them. Self-examination is not a spasmodic exercise undertaken during an occasional uprush of religious fervour but is made regularly with sensible method, for knowledge of myself is the foundation-stone of the building of detachment; as I change through the years so will my methods alter. And how different we all are; in the endless variety of temperaments there are those who need to deny themselves through action, others through negation; some to loosen the grasp, others to tighten it, these to compel, those to restrain. Am I impulsive, hasty, eager, my blood racing as I feel urged to put this right, get that done, arrange, organise, accomplish most in the least time? Or do I dislike asserting myself, preferring always to take the line of least resistance and, not so much meek and gentle as lethargic, refrain from disturbing the comfort of the situation because opposition and discord are painful? It can be so much easier

DETACHMENT

to refuse responsibility, not merely in respect of important activities but in such every-day matters as punctuality, tidiness and social courtesy. It is according to the nature with which we are born that we plan our self-denials: the ancient philosophers discerned wisely in their analysis of the four classical temperaments basic to humanity. Whichever is my foundation makes no difference to the necessity of freeing myself from my natural inclinations and forsaking my faults so that I may take a place just and fair within life's relationships, both giving and requiring the respect and deference they require and regulating all things in love and charity. We really do long to love God and respond to the immensity of divine Love that never ceases to surround, uphold and invite us, we want this more than we think we do; but our love grows step by step with our knowledge of Him, which itself both requires and gives a knowledge of ourselves: you cannot separate light and heat from fire. My business is to shape the stuff of myself, so I must know it.

It is the Religious who more than anyone effectively demonstrates the blessedness of the state of detachment in regard to possessions, people and self. The vow of poverty requires him to live with only the bare necessities for healthy life and service, with a frugal minimum of material goods. Quite apart from the freedom this gives to serve God and the church without ties and hindrances, this voluntary deprivation of the comforts and conditions which many people would call essential, the constant refusal of what both mind and body would naturally enjoy, all give the soul a lovely freedom and strength to yearn for God alone, disposing it to possess Him. There is an exaltation in voluntary poverty. (Perhaps we also need the gipsy and the tramp who, in a different category and on a lower level, exalt a freedom gained only by a denial of superfluity and security.)

The life of the monk or nun within a spiritual family functioning within the great family which is the church, demonstrates the reasonableness, power and joy of even deeper levels of denial undertaken in abstention from the normal life of human love and its organic expression and fulfilment, from all created ties of relationship. Detached from the natural sphere of passion, the desires and satisfactions common to all men, their love is not killed but supernaturalised, until its heights and depths embrace all men; and if one should fail to grow in this charity of grace, he may well become less a man than the beggar at the convent door, for he will have neither grace nor nature. But the love of charity differs from natural love as a mountain differs from a hill: and it is a necessity for us all. The Religious vow of obedience witnesses to the truth of Christ's word that whoever loses his life shall find it, for in the renunciation of will and its subjection to that of their Rule and their Superior (whom they voluntarily choose), monks and nuns, friars and sisters, find the surest, straightest road to union with the will of God; and it is undertaken only to follow their Master's example of total obedience to that same will. They are unconditionally at the disposal of God and so at the disposal of all men, therefore inevitably they are bound to be not only indomitable intercessors but to live lives of intercession: this through their self-emptiness.

> *He who binds to himself a joy*
> *Does the wingèd life destroy.*

They bind nothing to themselves, they are bound in Christ to the will of God, so they possess all things: even suffering. All, all is assumed for love, in love. We cannot do without their massive example of what is the foundation, the core and the continuance of all Christian life, and in the spiritual organism of the church we are sharers with them, as they with us, of the way and the fulfilment of sacrifice.

But for the majority of Christians the world is here for use, to be worked in, struggled with, rejoiced in, all of which is fruitfully possible and redemptively necessary only so far as we are free from it, free that is of possessiveness in regard to things, places, persons and ourselves: free to love. If the state of self-emptying, described, you may think, *ad nauseam*, were offered and chosen for its own sake it would indeed be a negative and cruel state; but it is desired and achieved, as far as I am able, only so that God the Blessed Trinity shall find in me the place prepared for Himself, the place which is rightly His, which from eternity He creates; so that I may be able to receive the charity of the Godhead with which I may love to eternity. Because this is the divine design I have confidence that God the Spirit will Himself teach me how to apply myself to the life-long process of detachment, lead me to play the game of memory—shut-the-door so that there are no engrossing images to arouse and minister to my vanity and pride, my resentments and cravings, no imaginations to assault my senses and build fancy pleasures and satisfactions, but a pure unity of heart, mind and will which rejoices in every showing of glory wherever it shines.

REDEMPTION

Inside the large, gaunt church of the small Spanish village, quietly dim against the brilliant light outside, I watched the little old woman. Black-dressed and shrivelled, she walked up the aisle to the nearly life-size crucifix which hung against the wall, she climbed the three steps into the alcove so that, reaching out, she could caress the feet. Gently, without haste, with deliberation, her fingers travelled over the image: a concentration of emotion seemed to flow out from her to the crucified. What was filling her heart? On another day I watched the life of the industrial city. There was no doubt about the intensity of purpose which drew the hundreds of men and women of all ages and types into the great cathedral, to join the ordered queue which moved slowly forward to the chapel where the centuries-old Lepanto crucifix was especially venerated on Lenten Fridays. What, I wondered, as again I watched, what did the Spanish mothers tell their pretty little girls whom they brought into the ancient hospital chapel of the Precious Blood, there to kneel in front of a much-loved crucifix; the figure small, realistic with its long real hair, adorned with the richly embroidered apron peculiar to Spain.

Many explanations can be offered for the deep and living devotion of so many people to the crucifix, but undergirding them all there must be a sense of relationship between their ordinary common trials and griefs and the pains of the crucified

God-Man. Not of some remote and abstract salvation were those people thinking but of Someone whose sufferings, made vivid by their representations in art, were actually helping them now in their endurance of present hardships, a Person who because of His pains was truly a very present help in time of trouble. And something more is required of me than the deliberate cultivation of faith, detachment and thanksgiving towards the wounds which life inflicts, I have to learn how those of Jesus Christ which are love-deep actually touch mine which are sin-deep. There is a life-giving exchange between us, between my Incarnate Lord and my poor, cold, disobedient self, not only because once in time, by what may seem to be a remote action, He redeemed me by a sacrificial death but in that His sufferings, then endured, touch mine and engulf them to-day, transmitting to me their transforming power and creative values. How can this be? We must try to explore the mystery as far as our weakness permits.

Throughout the ages an endless succession of men and women have suffered and died for truth, and we treasure the accounts of their great and noble deaths which fire our imagination and stir our desires to emulate them. The examples of Socrates, John the Baptist, Thomas More, Florence Nightingale and countless others are precious and serve to raise our eyes from the mean and selfish to the great and grand. Beyond this inspirational value, what can they of themselves effect? I admire and am humbly grateful for the shining splendour of their heroism and for their display of the glory of human conduct, and I believe that within the unity of human nature runs the shuttle of men's behaviour weaving us all into a pattern of interdependence. But I cannot now put my fears of life and death into their keeping and know that from them I shall receive what I sorely need, the virtues of trust and fortitude;

in no way can I actively relate my present sufferings with their long-past mortal miseries and travails, nor can I get from them comfort or gifts of grace, for they were finite as I am, limited to their years as regards their personal relationships (though not limited, it must be added, in the matter of timeless prayer in the heavenly kingdom). But very different are the sufferings of our Lord for, though endured by the man Jesus within the confines of actual human nature and according to its properties, they are infinite and everlasting in value and application because His human nature was once and forever knit indivisibly with the divine. Godhead and manhood meet in one Centre, one Self, in the Person of the Word who takes flesh. Nothing, therefore, within the eternal spirit of Christ is ever ended, the dispositions and workings of the Lord Jesus are as operative as those of the Second Person of the Trinity, for Jesus is God. So, the intentions and the virtues which filled His sufferings are as active, living and available at this moment as at any other. If He is alive for evermore and with us to the end of the world, so are the wounds of love which He came expressly to bear, the burden which He is everlastingly showing within the Godhead. Through the union which Christ gives me with Himself, by will and intention I join my sufferings to His and thereby draw into myself, receive from them, the grace which fills them, the virtue with which they are charged. All Christ's sufferings were acts of obedience to the Father constrained by mighty love and overflowing intensity of purpose to save mankind from the effects of its sinhood. Joined with His, my puny pains also can become acts of obedience, love and intercession, joined with His, I receive the virtues which informed them, His patience, His forbearance, fortitude, quietness, according to the measure of my soul to let suffering effect its purpose in me. Joined with His, mine also can become sacrifices, offerings of devotion, taken into the immensity of that divine act of interiorisation on the cross when Man offered to God the sacrifice of His whole pure self in love, the first and last true sacrifice.

This is possibly not what my worshippers in the Spanish churches were thinking, or perhaps even could think, but they were acting it, thereby teaching me to think. The personal application of the gospel of redemption is plainly made a living issue through the relationship of suffering. On my part I can use my pains as hands stretched out to Jesus our Lord, and it is because I know that His stretch down to me, that they are there first, before mine, that a possession of glory becomes apparent. Reasoning cannot of itself and unaided give me this knowledge, it requires to be clothed with the heart's devotion to the Person of the Redeemer; yet for the simple, the heart alone may be enough, which is what children learn.

Is it because their accent falls so heavily on the relevance of Christ's passion for suffering humanity that the churches made and used images of an agonised figure, realistic in physical anguish, images now so distasteful to many people? The early wood-carvings have such restraint and stillness, perhaps passivity, though not without triumph; only later did these become the twisted, tortured bodies which emphasise all the horror of the inflictions. Perhaps these are necessary to certain minds and at certain times, to demonstrate that the Saviour's agony is immense enough to absorb the suffering of every man, to underline His life-giving communion of anguish, to make plain His merciful love. Sometimes all aspects of the crucified Lord are wonderfully present in one representation, when the blood and the sweat, the wounds and the dyingness are there undisguised, but also the power, the oblation, the stillness and nobility; such a work is of special genius and grace, and through it Christ's sufferings are displayed as a dual road of approach, from Him to us, from us to Him.

It is right for the blood to remain, it should not be disguised for it cannot be forgotten, but it is not an end in itself. It is there to clothe and to display an energy of love; it is the outward sign of the sublime act of interiorisation which declares that the fullness of sacrifice is love. Man's faculty of thinking may continue to develop to astonishing levels, his powers of living inwardly and of possessing himself in abstraction from things may increase, but we shall always exist in our physical bodies, without which we cannot begin to imagine an earthly life, for it would be no longer this world. Indeed, it is the wonder and glory of creation that man is both soul and body and that neither can exist here without the other. The mode of their unity is beyond our comprehension, we have to accept the truth that each requires the other, that neither one is wholly itself without the other. A problem so fundamental (and fascinating) as the relationship between soul and body, inseparable as they are from their generation, has engaged man's ardent attention from the beginnings of serious thought, and inevitably there has been a continuous wrestling with opposing and fluctuating theories. The pre-eminence and importance of one element of being over another is either exaggerated or denied, and the swinging of the pendulum of thought from one unorthodox tenet to another produces errors which continue their influence on practical Christian living. It is as fatally easy and dangerous to be hyper-spiritual as to be materialistic, and both trends can be seen in the history of Christian religion. Yet it is through the strife of conflicting views that knowledge is deepened and truth apprehended more clearly; through the excesses of the few comes the balance of the many. Is there, perhaps, to-day an unhealthy dichotomy between body and soul? We Christians have the authority of the scriptures for our belief that man is man because it is his nature to be this composite and dangerously balanced creature; which is in fact the ground for our credal article of faith in the resurrection of the body, for, though the final body which we may win shall be spiritual and incorruptible, it is as something other than pure spirit that man inherits the ultimate kingdom of God.

So here in this life we cannot abolish nor should we shrink from the Precious Blood; there is something amiss when Christians dislike reference to it in prayers. A personal blood-shedding is often a shock, usually an unpleasantness, even though it be only from a violent nose-bleed or a cut finger. Why is this? To see the warm red liquid pulsing out, refusing to be staunched, may alarm just because it is one of the great physical mysteries of life, for as blood represents man's life so the person's existence seems involved in this draining. Who can make blood? It is the universal belief of antiquity and of all primitive people, as it is of the scriptures, that blood and life are synonymous. If the blood contains the life, the soul, it is therefore something to be reverenced, for it must belong especially to its Creator and is therefore sacred; and the heart being the fountain of blood and its peculiar organ shares in its importance. So we see that blood is of the essence of sacrifice and of covenant, for it is the offering of life. Whatever reason may impel the offering there can be no greater gift than that of one's own life, as our Lord declared when He said that no man can show greater love than in laying down his life. In saying this He joined together His own laying-down of His life on the cross and love. Blood, sacrifice, love—they are indivisible in the Incarnation, in our redemption, in devotion. Christ laid down His life in the out-pouring of His blood and thus the divine Priest and Victim fulfilled literally the requirements of the Old Covenant sacrifices which He brought to an end, for it was not in the death *qua* death that the sacrifice lay, but in the flowing of the blood which is the seat and principle of life. In the ancient sacrifices the great vein or the heart of the victim was pierced so that the live blood could be offered upon the altar: the actual body might be eaten by priests and people, for it held no sacrificial significance and was valuable only in a special sense of consecration, which drew the worshipper into a blessedness of communion with His God. 'The Lamb of God,' He is acclaimed by the first Saint John, as He begins His work: the 'Blood of the Lamb' is the mark, the seal, the very reason of the multitude beyond number who are God's worshippers in heaven, says another Saint John in his Apocalypse. The apostles, the first fathers of the church, and all their true successors have taught that man's salvation is effected through the Blood of Jesus: the blood means the crucifix, the Passion, suffering. Blessed be the most Precious Blood of Jesus.

At no time has the religion of the English people been expressed with greater simplicity, more tenderness or more intimate love than from roughly the end of the thirteenth century for a period of two hundred years. There was then a succession of notable men and women, mostly priests and Religious, whose range of knowledge, depth of devotion and competent, even poetic skill in expression, produced a number of spiritual books of such excellent quality that they became classics for all time, the nourishment of souls today, such as those of Walter Hilton, Richard Rolle, Dame Julian of Norwich, Nicholas Love, with the addition of some anonymous writings. Their common and outstanding characteristic is their fervent devotion to the Person of our Lord Jesus Christ, which inevitably was accompanied by great reverence and sympathy

REDEMPTION

for His Blessed Mother, for His gift of Himself in the blessed sacrament, but above all, for His cross and Passion. It is evident from the great number of poems, songs and carols preserved in mediaeval manuscripts, the majority of which are anonymous, that the Person of Jesus Christ was the heart and mainspring of the religion not only of the educated minority and, we might say, of the professional ecclesiastics, but of all the common people. That they have been preserved in their anonymity like folk-ballads, without the influence and the art of well-known literary names, shows how spontaneously and truly they expressed the mind of the people of the villages and towns equally with the inhabitants of monasteries; they were really popular. Like folk-songs, there is constant recurrence of the same expressions, the same images, which do not weary because they are both taut and simple, and this is very noticeable in the poetry of the Passion. What the verse-makers with their concrete vision are concerned to display are the few great acts of the sacred drama, their reason and necessity and the response they must elicit; and what the carved crucifix does silently, the poems demand clearly—they ask for love to answer Love.

Perhaps Our Lord Himself speaks.

> *Behold, O man, lift up thine eye and see*
> *What mortal pain I suffered for thy trespass;*
> *How that I, to bring thee back to grace,*
> *Was like a lamb offered in sacrifice.*

and:

> *Upon a cross nailed I was for thee*
> *and suffered death to pay thy ransom.*
> *Forsake thy sin: I gave my life for thee.*

Behold my love, and give Me thine.

*Jesus Who died on the Rood for love of me
And bought me with Thy precious blood,
Have mercy on me.*

It is as simple as that. Jesus by His blood-shedding to death has bought me, therefore, I must love and serve Him. There is a deep and perpetual bond between us, because He has bought me, therefore, how should I not love?

*Jesu, God's only Son Thou art,
Lord of high majesty,
Send Thy true love into mine heart,
Only to covet Thee.*

Such poetry is native to us, our heritage: and so also is the sign of our saving. There were the tall crosses in the market-squares or churchyards, where the wandering friars and the peripatetic hermits preached, there were the crosses over the moors which marked the pathways from one big monastery to another, there were the crucifixes sculptured above or at the side of the south porches of village churches, or painted in glowing glass in the great conventual churches and the cathedrals; and they all said, 'for love'. And love wants to look. 'Behold,' says Christ, 'behold and see my wounds, my bloody face, my side.'

What to-day do we make of those lines, 'I died thy ransom to pay', or, 'My ransom sure He offered there', or 'Upon a Cross, our souls to buy, He died.' From whom does He buy? Whose prisoner was I? Those who made the songs and wrote the poems did not apparently ask; they accepted the great deed of the mighty Lord and wanted men to answer it by forsaking sin and loving Him with all their heart, soul and strength. To show the way to this love was what the writers of our English spiritual classics essayed, in language unrivalled for its freshness, homeliness and dignity, in a style unsurpassed for naturalness, lucidity and beauty. Will a day come when once again we crowd round the preacher, the conductor, the director, to press home our questions, 'How can we love perfectly?' 'How can we know Him better, He who asks for love? Do not put us off with emptiness of exhortation, composed platitudes of the head, give us of the heart and drive us to doing.' Though the idea of our souls being bought, or being ransomed, has perhaps become alien to contemporary thinking, yet it was Jesus' idea, for He announced that He came to be a ransom. One day, when for me there will be no more days, I shall see Him; what will be my shame, what will be my sorrow, my undoing, if I do not know something of what He said He came to do for me?

Does the unhasting, everlasting song of the redeemed which sounds through the heavenlies rise from the hearts of creatures who have received into their being a complete knowledge of the work of their Redeemer Christ, the Lamb of God, and does their mirth spring from minds which see all? Can God show to that which is not God the fullness of the mystery which He as man achieved for creation? We do not know, but we may be sure that when at last the doors of eternity open to us, our spiritual eyes will see beyond anything we can now imagine: knowledge will accompany sight, and love surpassing reason will carry us on to the place prepared for us. Love is the end of the beginning, and although in this life our spiritual knowledge is at best clouded and fragmentary, yet it must be enough to set fire to love, through which it becomes itself enlarged. That which took place in the particular moment of the Passion was—better, perhaps, to say is—so vast, so colossal, so supernatural, with values so comprehensive and central, that none of the speculations and theories advanced by Christian thinkers has ever been able to embrace them all: the church has never imposed on its members a credal closed account of the atonement. The mystery must be accepted and rejoiced in, whilst the mind must ever try, within both its limits and scriptural exposition, to understand what underlies experience. How our salvation was procured is beyond the reach of human reason but not at all beyond human adoration and thanksgiving. And in this we get nowhere, nowhere at all, without recognition of sin, a personal and subjective cognisance and not merely an objective and abstract perception; a recognition which is accompanied by a hatred and dread of it as moral evil, perhaps the only evil; and of this evil suffering is the inevitable effect and shadow.

That I have been bought and ransomed infers that I was in a condition of belonging otherwise than to myself, that I was without freedom, not my own agent but tied to a contrary power; and that describes the state of sin. Sin it is which makes me unable to live according to my true nature, which chains and binds me to what is antagonistic to the fulfilment of my end and the purpose of my being. Through sin I am not what I am meant to be, I am missing my true goal, I am twisted out of shape so that I am not facing the right way. Sin is like a poison in my bloodstream circulating through my body which is all affected; it is alien, untrue, and I cannot rid myself of it; the evil possesses me. What is my true state of being as God designed me, the end for which He made me? It is to be wholly centred upon Him who contains all, and so to find in Him my joy and delight, my peace, my plan. This does not mean that I begin by isolating Him to the exclusion of His creation. The kingdom of this world is mine and for me, its people with souls and bodies, their arts and sciences, their life, motion, rest; I do not ignore that kingdom, despise or refuse it. All that it offers is for my use, but it is to be desired and enjoyed in God and not for its own sake, for it has nothing of its own, nor for my sake, for I am nothing apart from Him. All is in conscious dependence upon the Creator and Fount of all life who is Life, and, therefore, all exists in interdependence, abiding in an unbroken response to the adorable Majesty, a response which is love: and even that love is the gift of Himself who is essentially Love. Is this how I live, how all men live? Not so: I am not like that, for I am wrapped around myself, and mankind turns to itself. I want this and this and this for myself and for my benefit, and I want them to excess and at any price, even the price of my own and my neighbour's health, happiness, peace, even his life. Or perhaps I cannot be bothered to want or make use of anything, to the neglect of all my faculties and the repudiation of responsibilities. One way or another, my will resists God's law, natural and revealed, law which is the expression in practical commandments of His own Nature and therefore neither arbitrary nor extrinsic but the very revelation of His Being and the good health of my own. For even though I, being a law unto myself, may hate, I may steal, lie, destroy, none of this brings me health nor joy.

This is the condition of all humanity, yet all men have within them a seed of yearning to be other than they are. None are wholly contented, for however much they may live to please themselves they do not possess themselves. At least sometimes (for an inner light, a conscience is denied to no one) I know what is my real good, what is right and what is of love, and I am aware of the foolishness and insufficiency of my behaviour, of my meanness; yet though I desire to alter, I find I cannot control the interior principle and contradiction which splits my being: I do what I don't mean to do, I can't be what I wish. I have chosen evil and the thing which is evil has me in thrall. I don't know, I can't see, whether my happiness lies in this action or in that: O, that I knew! O my sinhood! Yet though it displeases me that I am thus tied up, caught in a bondage of beastliness, there remains a part of me which, being involved in that which is nevertheless despised, is too weak to be truly sorry, too ill to make the effort to be well, too lethargic to break the ties. It has got to be done for me, I must be bought, ransomed. Yet I must myself be involved in the doing or it will not be I myself, a person of will and desires, who is remade, restored to my native state.

It is as if man were a planet revolving round its sun of Glory and fount of life, the true and only centre of its attraction, which maintains it in safety, stability, order. This planet, which was man, chose, having been created with a power of choice (unlike the solar systems of the universe which we accept as mechanical), to break away from its ordered path of attraction and bound off at a tangent from its natural orbit. The guiding gravity of order is lost, and the momentum of its desired existence hurtles the planet farther and farther away into the darkness of outer space, into disordered motion, loss, perhaps final destruction. No inherent power of the careering body can restore it to its true orbit, only some fresh imposed mode of attraction will do this. So, our Sun, God in Trinity, provides my means of restoration from within Himself, so that once more I can freely revolve around Him. It cannot be otherwise than that as God in creating man endowed him with the power of choice, so in His omniscience He would provide the remedy for the effects of a wrong choice and for the overcoming of that reversal of good which is evil. Our Creator honoured us by giving us free-will (this great dignity of humankind, this beauty of our form), we abused this honourable trust, as God foresaw we should: yet to bring good out of evil is more god-like than to create a mechanical good, more in accordance with the wonder of omnipotence, and displays the divine nature in all its attributes of mercy not disjoined from justice and compassion, not separate from righteousness. From all eternity the Second Person of the Godhead wills to take to Himself human nature, and within that nature, yet without denial of His divinity, He will by His eternal perfection break the contradiction and live in undivided simplicity, in wholeness. Because He offers complete obedience to the Creator whose purpose has fashioned mankind, the Incarnate Lord lives wholly free within the divine will. Here is a Person perfect in all ways as the Creator designed man to be, a Son who delights wholly in His Father and can give Him due honour worthy of His Immeasurable purity. But this perfection of human nature which is the instrument of God's Incarnation is not disjoined from the tainted, sin-riddled nature of all mankind, and, therefore, the Son's obedience is effected, matured, achieved, only in conflict with evil; this entails the endurance to its extreme limit of that suffering which is the effect and the inevitable end of sin, the limit of death. There is no other way in which evil can be defeated and its power destroyed, no other means but that of this sinless, human-divine sacrifice in which complete sorrow for all sin, and an unbroken will for communion with God all-Holy, Pure, Infinite, are maintained inviolable against all the force of evil. And all is done in love, for love. New life streams from those five precious wounds like the vibrant shafts of light through the ruby glass of the ancient windows. Jesus our Lord, how can we begin our thanking and our praising, which never can be enough? Our thanksgiving is in rejoicing in salvation and glory. Through this perfect restitution of what is due to the honour of the Creator, which sinful man with his warped will and darkened vision could never make, God communicates to us His forgiveness, restoring us to filial relationship with Him and opening to us His heaven, the place of light, peace, felicity.

But it is my nature which my Jesus assumed, my nature with all its sinhood and suffering, and it is within that that I am taken up into His offering, into that sacrificial obedience of His life and death which buys my forgiveness and restoration; and so it is that His intentions, His desires and His merits as perfect man can be communicated to me through the channel of human nature. This is no mechanical, formal transaction, for that would disregard God's creation of man as a free agent with a reasonable will; it would deny truth; it is effective only according to my faith, my obedience, my love, according to the energy with which I reject and resist evil temptations and the motions of sin. Grace is not imposed, it is offered, sufficient for all, free-flowing over all who make use of it. This new principle of life, this supernatural gift of restoration which is grace is the fruit of the Precious Blood of Jesus: we are back where we started from. As a lover delights to explore the depths of the personality of his beloved, seeking as a necessity of love to penetrate the full extent of its riches, so I must return again and again to these fundamental principles of our faith and profession, trying to grasp their meaning and see their relevance for practical life, which is a life of communion with God. And my path, as we have surely seen, will always come back to love, a love which is granite as well as honey, which demands as well as gives, which is suffering and glory, darkness and light, which is death as well as life. This is our truth.

REDEMPTION

Jesu, my only joy,
For all the gifts Thou givest me,
For the blood Thou shed'st for me,
For the Cross Thou bor'st for me,
Give Thou me grace to sing
The Song of thy Loving.

No wonder that we fall on our knees, in body as in spirit, in adoring awe at the words, "The Word became flesh and dwelt amongst us." In the growing immensities of this space-age there must be born anew the devotion to the one Person Jesus, who is circumference and centre. May the image of the divine sufferer be imprinted on my memory so that I am never left for long without the reminder of my total involvement with God, so that I am continually recalled to my part in sacrifice, in the offering of love.

What is the life of a persevering Christian if it is not a gradual but sure growth in sacrifice, in an unbroken offering? Each day provides the material of the offering, the thing to be surrendered or accepted by deliberate acts of will, which always finds a parallel in the offering made by our Lord, finds the likeness with which it can be joined. Nothing is too trivial as an offering so long as it costs something, no sort of suffering need be despised and considered too foolish, too insignificant for our Lord to see. The strange indispositions which defy diagnosis, the thickets of fear which invade and paralyse mind, heart and soul, the psychical malaise which changes a person's face, have all been felt by Jesus in the agony which preluded His Passion. Those little irritations of trifling incapacities, of carelessness, of mistakes, whether they are our own or other people's, are united to the patience and calm with which He endured them in His disciples and friends; the sore wounds which we receive from family and friends when we are misjudged, forgotten, scorned, unkindly treated, are already His. There is no range of loneliness, no misery of misunderstanding, no refusal of relationship, which Jesus has not suffered in the extreme, to which we can join our pains. For we have nothing of our own—all finds its value only in the pure spotless offering of Christ. No one has known more than He of the frustrations and blinding obtuseness of colleagues and followers, of the petty meanness of human nature's self-seeking, and also of that density of grief which comes from the necessity to give pain to those we love, to refuse them what seems their rights. Even our nightmares of doubt and uncertainty and monstrous accusation find their place in our Lord's woe.

A suffering there is which could seem to be outside His sympathy and beyond His ken, one that belongs peculiarly to sin-stricken man, and that is, the pain we carry of not being able to attain the vision we have seen, to respond to the call to holiness, to be simply good if not heroically saints. As we look back on the years we wonder whether they have brought us any increase in virtue: the same faults, weaknesses and failures stick out like spines on a hog. We bear a dull weight of self-awareness which may invade even our holiest moments and block our self-oblation, which prevents us from being wide open to the light that is of God, from abiding, self-forgotten, in that beatitude which is the sense of His presence. We can never lose the shadow of shame and sorrow which is ours because we daily fall short of our true stature as children of God as we sin against love. So penitence is our clothing. The perfect Son of God never knew what it was to sin, to grieve His Father and hurt His fellows, to be limited in holiness; Jesus who was Light alone knew God in His Essence and never for one instant failed to fulfil His word: how then can He know man's misery of failure? But, yes, He knew. Having taken sinful, impotent, deflected, human nature to Himself, He knew, He felt, He carried all its agonies. "My soul is exceeding sorrowful even unto death": not for anything that He had done or not done, but for my doing and my not-doing: in order to be my undoing and remaking. That sorrow to death is the perfect contrition of the Lord of creation whose purity made it possible for Him to see and assess the gravity of creation's stain, who alone could fully grieve over its malignity. His contrition then outran sin and outstripped the sight of sin, assuming into itself the anguish which is its penalty. As He alone can measure the awfulness of sin, its extent and its damage, so He only can be truly sorry for it; and only in and with His penitence are we truly sorry. He is not only the ultimate ground of the priest but also of the penitent; for it was as priest, victim, penitent that He hung upon the altar-cross around which blew the winds of eternity.

In the Sacrament of Penance, the redeeming power of His Precious Blood, which is throughout time ever available for the inward saving of all men, is brought into an expressed and definite relation with the individual. As we receive this concentration of spiritual power given to us by His mercy, we can interiorise our sufferings (not of course our sins) by an act of union with all those Christ bore for us. As we do this not only in general but in particular, with this and that tangible difficulty and trouble, we realise that they can all be used as actual means of reconciliation, elements in expiation and very real sacrifices: then we know that we could not do without them, for they are gifts from God to give back again to Him in a tide of love. And all this through the offering of the Lamb's Blood. Our sufferings are points of relevancy between Christ's Passion and our salvation, and therein His glory. Here, declares our Lord, here is my game with you. We can go no further with our sufferings than to take hold of them as best we may and hand them to our Lord Jesus, who will show them in the heavenlies, with the marks of His own, to the praise and joy and welcome of all the church triumphant: and the echo of that song will sound in our torn hearts, here and now. But, 'as best we may' implies a life-time of practice.

In the world of nature there seems to be immeasurable loss and waste, so much that is never realised, productive, completed for the part, even if the decay of the less appears to benefit the whole. But in the world of spirit this is not so, there nothing is wasted, useless, unprofitable: uselessness can be valuable, sterility fecund, emptiness be productive, for all should be caught up into the creative energy of sacrifice. Even in learning to see, say and believe that we are unprofitable servants we become fulfilled in truth. When by intention and will we unite our pains with our Lord's, placing them in the chalice of His Blood, they have a place within the creative process of redemption: which, though it springs from an operation accomplished and concluded in a past given moment, is co-equal with time running to and fro. Is there an operation more powerfully creative, more divinely archetectonic, more fruitful, than the re-creation of man, his restoration to his intended place in divine life, and his renewal in glory: except his original creation by Almighty God? In this mighty river of divine creation and re-creation there is no past and future, there is one everlastingness, into which we are plunged by our present. And only the mercy of Omnipotent God could foreordain the use of men's sufferings as an essential element in the divine comedy. If the argument which we have been steadily (and I can only hope, not ponderously) unfolding has validity and meaning, here we have reached its conclusion. "Ought not

REDEMPTION

Christ to suffer these things?" Then we ought also: and so to enter into His Glory.

But for me to accept and to assume suffering in union with our Lord's redeeming pains is one thing, there is the problem of that great and undeniably mysterious area of mental suffering in which countless individuals are held captive in a state of impotence of mind and will. The dreadful scenes of madness, the condition of complete senility, the pathetic emptying of the personality through dread disease, all reveal the invalid's incapacity for any directed spiritual movement or rational energy whatsoever. What of their passion? Dare we inquire into what are naturally called wasted lives? As a preliminary we must see that there cannot be divisions within the sphere of suffering, nor any stocktaking which will label some kinds as useful, credible, blessed, others as wicked, futile and barren, nor any distinction between the quality of pain, physical and mental. Suffering is indivisible, and only the concept of sacrifice will shed any light upon its mystery. None can deny that the principle of sacrifice is inherent in nature, that it runs through life like the grain in a section of wood. Without the offering of womb and blood there is no birth, each one of us is carried into the world on the shoulders of maternal sacrifice, and this at the beginning of life declares an essential element in all relationship. All sacrifice is purposeful and when it is not for one's personal benefit it is made on behalf of someone, it is vicarious. The hideous travesty of existence which shocks us in many hospital patients (whose condition we must remember is not personally realised and felt by them as we see and feel it) may be and surely is, vicarious. In the vast pattern of mankind's unity woven on the loom of life the criss-cross of threads will provide that the strange unaccountable disease born by one person is working out and atoning for the evil and rebellion of another, as was our Lord's agony and death which overcame evil and brought forgiveness for us all. When placed within the crucible of Christ's Passion there is no piece of pain that is not redemptive. God alone knows this mystery of vicarious redemption in which the pains of the innocent (yet, in the unity of kind, none is innocent) are drawn into the great sea of Christ's sacrifice and there find their purpose and their glory; but if Christ rejoiced to suffer for us, so, in their ultimate fruition and life of divine love, do they. One thing is sure, which is, that evil, dread, terrible, loathsome damned and damning evil, has to be paid for and to be worked out of the great system which is humankind, of which Christ is the Head. Any Christian who engages in prayer for others knows what it is to have the soul inundated with depression, heaviness, an almost tangible weight of pain, which is the effect of the sin and evil claiming place in the person being prayed for. It is a common experience for the whole man to be worn out by a very costly intercession. And as the spirit can thus suffer vicariously, so also may the body. We may never know whence comes the strain which causes an organic crack, but bodily troubles and disabilities may sometimes be explained by the spiritual sharing of burdens within the fellowship of Christ; and when this is so, restoration of health is more likely to be achieved by fortitude, calmness and complete dependence upon God than by any physical remedies. It is noteworthy that belief in efficacious vicarious suffering is expressed in the earliest known religious hymns of the human race, those of the Aryan Vedas. And as evil continues in time and space to assert its strength and work its damage in creation through men's sinful wills, so must sacrificial and redeeming suffering continue, tho' never disjoined from the timeless sorrow of the cross; suffering which both expresses and deepens repentance. Saint Paul repeatedly asserts that in the unity of the Body with its Head there is a fellowship with Christ's sufferings: and we must search out, as the Holy Spirit enlightens us, the meaning of that word fellowship, even if it takes us as far as a readiness to fill up what could be lacking in the Saviour's afflictions, which the apostle rejoiced to do. It may be that honour compels us to make our contribution, to add what we can to the already full treasury, that in the realisation of our debt, love and contrition are not satisfied until they share in suffering. Since the supreme revelation on the Cross of the measure of divine love, there have never been wanting souls whose response has been to pour out such an energy of answering love that their whole work and calling is to offer repentance for the unrepentant, contrition for all sin, love for those who do not love; hidden and unknown, they are living sacrifices for the conversion of the world. As such they stand. But there are several planes within the communion of suffering. To be bound with Christ upon His cross may be imposed upon many who do not know Him or their place there and who may even seem to lack the power to know: may be offered by the Spirit to the few whom in all ages He calls to the hidden life of reparation: may be humbly and thankfully accepted by every Christian in the daily experience of suffering, small and great.

Surely we are made aware of the creative power of pain by what it does for those who care for the afflicted. Any ministry of mercy unlocks the doors which reveal in all their strength and beauty unsuspected depths of compassion and sweetness, of competence and understanding, and this in persons who ordinarily appear to have little seriousness or depth of character. It is hard to imagine the blossoming of virtue without this world's estate of stress and distress, of tears and pain. 'Perfect through suffering': a mystery of truth.

DOORS OF ETERNITY

*And when God formed in the hollow of His Hand
This planet Earth among his other spheres...
He chose it for the Star of suffering.**

And all the stars shined in their watches and rejoiced.

---

* *Facing Pain,* Hamilton King's Hospital Sermon, ed. by a member of the Community of the Resurrection.

SEPARATION

What is the metaphysical heart of suffering? Could it be division, separation? When am I aware of pain? When I am separated from normal health of body, mind or spirit, when I am divided from that which is vital and important to my well-being, deprived of that which satisfies me as good, whether it be a true good or what I suppose to be good. 'True' is probably the right and conclusive word for that which is true to the creature's essential nature contributes to its wholeness, its fulfilment, to what it is substantially meant to be: therefore to happiness. It is true for a chair to have its seat, the bird its wings, the camel its hump, true for men to have eyes, memory, marriage, for a Christian to have faith, penitence, joy. And to be all true is to be fulfilled, to have attained unity, to be in peace. To be separated from the truth of one's being is the ultimate cause of suffering.

The philosophy which underlies the great Eastern religions, notably that of Buddhism, holds that life is sorrow, suffering and decay largely through lack of correspondence between desire and satisfaction; therefore to achieve peace and calmness there must be cessation of all desire. Complete detachment is the only path of contentment. Though this may appear to find an exact parallel in many of our Lord's injunctions, its reason and its end are radically different. If such detachment is followed to its conclusion it entails contracting out of life, logically it annihilates love (though in practice the Buddhist laws enjoin compassion and kindness). And it can make no sense of the mystery of suffering nor relate it to a God of Love.

Often it is our necessity and our duty passionately to desire something for ourselves or for others, and to suffer accordingly when it is not forthcoming. This is part of the process of growth and of struggle for fulfilment and perfection, and so long as I am short of my full stature, all my life is growth. The separation which causes suffering is not always due to negation, to the absence or withdrawal of a possessed good, to a broken relationship. It may derive from a condition of growth, in which case it has a positive content. Whilst the young child is growing the equipment of teeth which belong to the next stage of its maturity it suffers alarmingly (and so do others!), yet until those teeth are in place its organism lacks finish and is separated from normality; the growth is healthy, the pain inevitable (and soon forgotten). But disorderly growth may appear in any part of the body and foster division to the point of decay, being physically negative; disorderly growth may appear in the psyche, to be an alarming instrument of separation from sound and balanced life: and all this is aberration. Normal growth, whatever the cost, is thrilling and exhilarating like the struggle in any sport, for it looks forward to a state of completeness and fulfilment. In fact, it is impossible to consider the notions of separation and growth apart from each other: and this, if we make a metaphorical leap up the ladder of our subject, confronts us with the paradox which we are constantly glimpsing, that the experiences of suffering and joy are not antagonistic but are only fully known in synthesis and within a bond of unity.

My life both outward and inward is one long striving to attain my full stature, a struggle to overcome and remove that

SEPARATION

which divides me from fruition, to satisfy my desires for the fullest good as I know it. In the body this will be attended by slow beginnings of decay which, as these increase without any accompanying renewals, will bring new forms of separation from wholeness; and so we are caught (as the Buddhist maintains) in a cycle of becoming and diminishing. In the spirit, however, this is not so: there is change but no decay, there is diminishing which proves to be enlargement, and the processes of separation, detachment and progressive emptying generate unity, achieve a drawing-together of the parts into a whole in which all desires are satisfied without any sense of loss. This, however, is our end, an end realised above, beyond and outside ourselves. Life is the overcoming and assimilation of the necessary condition of separation through the suffering of acceptance.

In the beginning God by the division of chaos ordained creative rhythm, and the principle of division which marks all time and all existence becomes a law of life. If it is a law of life it cannot in itself be evil though it may be an agony; by its very nature as divine law it must be productive of joy and of glory and be the vehicle of love; and we discern and receive this to be true only within the reaches of experience which we make fully our own in the costly process of acceptance, which is, as we have continually argued, the practice of self-denial to which we are Christianly committed. In spiritual geometry there is no straight line which is not part of a circle. This law operates from our birth. It is through an experience of separation that the child probably receives his first recollected awareness of emotional pain, a pain which reaches down to the roots of his psyche and so disturbs his whole being. A young child can be so overwhelmed by the grief of a sudden removal of one who has been its constant and beloved companion, that it becomes incapable of responding to the business of living; its sorrow absorbs all its faculties and drains away the energy of its will, and it cannot lift itself above it nor be distracted from it. With a highly-strung and sensitive nature this state may become desperate: there have been instances when, in the absence of human salvation, God's compassion has provided a heavenly visitor to bring a measure of tranquillity and ensure the gentle restoration of existential well-being. In its immaturity a child's memory is normally short and recovery will leave no ugly scar, though the wound may reopen if it has not wholly healed. Once to have witnessed the extent to which a small child can suffer through the sudden removal of a parent who has been an essential part of its daily life lifts the lid from a well of pain so deep that memory cannot lose the sight. Yet such affliction is unavoidable in this world as it is, where fault and mistake must continually enmesh the innocent.

Perhaps it is fear of and shrinking from inevitable heart-sickness which determine some people to withdraw as far as possible from the conditions and commitments of social relationship. They embark on wholesome intimacies but resolutely refuse to continue when there are signs of tensions, unforeseen clouds and unknown storms, all inevitable in the nature of things. But this refusal, if conscious and persistent, must be at the expense of love, love the ultimate principle of life and the condition of each soul's growth and fulfilment. Life is built on separation, physical, psychical, emotional, spiritual, established as it is in the roots of being: and love which is the power that draws together and unifies is itself the ground of our experience that this separation between those in close communion brings our deepest suffering.

And so on through the growing years and into maturity there is for most of us a succession of normal experiences of

SEPARATION

parting and losses, cruel and harrowing at the time, beyond, we think, our power to sustain and recover. "I shall never be the same again" is the common cry, which is probably true, though not in the despairing sense we mean; for each circumstance hung on the loom of life has its purpose in preparing the sufferer to know and to find his soul as he loses himself. They are personal gifts, these episodes of loss, which can be either spurned or used, scorned or treasured; to take, use and treasure may, probably will, bring more suffering than would rejection: but the suffering is that which will actually enrich and strengthen life and be the cause of peace and final joy. To say this does not mean that pain is not really felt, that it evaporates and can be disregarded—far from it; it means that it becomes a point of revelation. The world indeed rocks with the anguish of division, and we rock. Surely the heaviest woe of war is not the killings nor the cruelties nor the ravages of physical and mental wounds but the anguish of separation which pervades the whole operation, from which few can escape. War, like slavery, is persecution, is a crescendo of fracture on a gigantic scale, far beyond the power of men to anneal, mend or sanctify; though we do not doubt that the immensity of its suffering weighs in the balance against the black evil which purposes to sway mankind to destruction. That is displayed by the cross.

Many of the finest and most noble lines of the world's literature, which quickly touch the deep springs and open the floodgates, are concerned with the universal theme of farewell. The great poetry of all the centuries holds the secrets of the broken heart; it speaks of the deep sorrows of parting, of the empty place, the yearning to see again the lost face and to hear the voice crying on the wind: all of which is as common to us as breathing. We did not have to wait for the revelations of Christianity to receive the truth that pain and joy are simultaneous in the experience of love. More than anyone the poet (and a part of the poet may be in any one of us) yearns intensely to find and feel the unity of life; and this therefore makes him more vulnerable to the bitterness and sadness of the disunion which he is impelled to unfold and expose. He exposes it for us all. We do not have to call many years our own before we begin to sense that existence holds deep pools of painful solitariness and waters of strange loneliness, although we have no words to express this, nor understanding of its significance. Adolescence is a difficult and inconclusive stage in life, marked by bewildering moods which suddenly come upon the teenager and the maturing youth, moods which cannot be explained or related to experience and which shatter emotional stability. These disturbances are warnings and previews of the uncrossable spaces which divide person from person, even when there are strong bonds of love and sympathy. This is the time when first we begin to feel that we are different from others, when a person realises that there are tracts of his personality peculiar to himself, unrecognised by others and unable to be shared with them. This isolation can hurt: will it last forever? Perhaps one day there will come the perfect mate, someone who will share completely, to whom everything can be revealed and who in turn will yield all secrets: with such a one, enlargement and fruition will mean unbroken happiness.

"Dear, I would show you all my heart's desires,
The anguished yearning of my spirit's need of your dear presence."

But, alas, experience discovers a tract of spiritual isolation as real and unyielding as any physical desert. However strongly two people are drawn together in love, whatever the range of their shared sympathies and pursuits and the depths of their

SEPARATION

common beliefs, the unity which they build and maintain neither nullifies nor bridges the disparateness of two individuals. Each is always essentially itself in a realm of I-ness which cannot either disclose itself or receive the full disclosure of the other. "Inthronging one another we ever fail to find each other": a double pain. This vast and deep solitariness is inherent and is, therefore, an ontological suffering. It is perceived and experienced only in the context of closest relationship, when the isolation of the one is floodlit by the real union of the two. Love draws attention to the walls of solitude which divide. As usual we arrive at the threshold of paradox: I cannot think of myself apart from people, for love is my nature and my nature is love, and it follows that I am the more myself the more I am directed towards others; yet though I carry within me an emptiness which cries out to be filled, I can never have it satisfied by a perfection of communion with them. I do all I can to bridge the gulf which exists between us, I do not accept it or allow for it until I have worked with all the powers of my being both to give and to receive to the uttermost, to be wholly accessible; but the unknowable remains, and aloneness has the victory. The chief pain of love is never to be able to love enough: there is its finitude. We have to accede to spiritual loneliness; it is provided by God Himself and, therefore, must be good. If I refuse to acknowledge and to prepare for it, I keep Him out: so I shall not be fulfilled in love.

This is not to deny or diminish the unmeasured depths of unity achieved by those who love, for it is the prerogative of true love to reach down into the very roots of being. What is going, then, to happen to me when we are torn apart for ever in this world? we who are made for each other, who have through the years grown into a unity? I cannot believe that it will ever happen, that it can ever be our lot to be separated; it would be a pain too vast to be borne. Do not ever go, beloved, do not ever die. If a fear comes that you could, that you might, I will refuse it, it shall be buried, deep: that fear of the void of death, I will not know it. But it comes, it comes, the day of severance and you are gone by a sudden lift of the hand of God. You are not here, nor ever will be again. At first I am lifted with you, in an overmastering sense of presentation, as if for a second time our troth is plighted at a heavenly altar. God wraps me in His shining mercy as a child is wrapped in a shawl, round and round. You are gone on into its beauty, and this must be. But when there is no longer the reflection of the shining brightness of your swift flight, I go on into gloom. As I drive away up the high hill above the mist-filled valley there rises suddenly out of a bank of thin fog the most part of a pale-gold sun, which sprays with clear light a long tendril of dark cloud above it. So, you are gone on into golden light, but I must descend into winter's fog and in fog drive on alone, into the darkness of night.

Comes now the day and the moment of unimagined agony, when something within is broken forever, and even the ability to look towards God and receive His grace and strength is gone. Sheer emptiness, lonely ways, stretching on all sides, everything dark, cold, hopeless, closing in on me like thick fog. No light, no strength, only a voiceless gloom. This, this is the hour of desolation, and there is no escape and no relief. O God, what shall I do? I cannot bear it, this black agony, this utter loneliness, together with the loss of fortitude. What is blocking the way to the strength which God promises to give? Is it self-pity, complaint? Are the emotions trying to drag me into their clamour for satisfaction? The answer must lie in my use of the agony, from which I will not turn away, even if I could. There is no quick anodyne, nor should there be. I am stripped and

SEPARATION

there is not even vinegar offered for my drinking. The suffering is my entry into sacrifice and must become my offering. "Father, into Thy Hands I commend this." But how can I say it?

I am like an animal caught in a trap, there is no way to turn without increasing the pain. If I remain alone, when I am in solitude, when there comes the hour of night, I am filled with the images of my lost love, I dwell upon all the causes and sequence of my grief until my head aches beyond relief: nor is there any power to find rest in God. If I go to seek companionship, I am uncertain whether I can control myself and I shrink from people; I am an open wound which bleeds anew at the slightest touch. I should like to go to the right person, if I knew who it is, and simply give way to grief; surely I could be saved by breaking down without reserve or moderation? But no, that sort of display is a travesty of true grief; there is an indignity about uncontrolled distress, for none is uncontrollable if one is full-grown. Grief without silence and without restraint diminishes me and will remove me from God as surely as deliberate sin; in fact its roots are in sin because it is a self-seeking and not a true self-emptying. It is another matter should God send a saviour to me. No, I must act: therein lies relief. I will turn to any sort of activity, any task which requires attention; the most ordinary manual labour is good. I must go and do something for someone, with deliberation, go forth with outwardness in my gesture and intention, put myself resolutely at the disposal of those around me. Whole-heartedly, was I going to say? I have no whole heart. No, but I have a will: and I must force my thoughts away from you, beloved, you who are filling so exclusively the periphery of my mind. Of what use are the years of discipline, self-denial and practised detachment if I cannot now order my thoughts? When your image fills my memory I will answer it by thanksgiving: thanks for all you gave me, what you meant to me, what you were, thanks for our lovely life together, given to us by God; so, thanks it is to God, and blessing Him for His gifts must lead on to blessing Him for Himself. And for you in Him: and that none else can do as I can, because I alone know you wholly. There will be something missing from the song of the heavenlies if I do not thank God for you and for you in Him. And this way lies relief and salvation.

I see very plainly, O my God, that I do myself no good if I allow my imagination its facility to see my beloved here and there in the familiar places, with the well-known gestures, the customary manners. It seems as if I have only to turn my head and I shall see you coming, to put out a hand and you, my dear, will take it; you are almost bound to materialise. But how foolish and how lowering to man's true nature to continue clinging to the vanished vision. Of course memory turns back to dwell upon that which was the other half of myself, but I must check it, gently and persistently picking up the thoughts, as it were, and moving them onwards: like the insistent removal of the cat from the chair where it is determined to sleep, though I am determined that it shall not. I win, but not if I leave the chair empty. All the time my positive assertion is that in God my beloved is as truly alive and as certain a real person as he was in his flesh and more so: and so there is no separation. This, not visual recalling, is what must fill my thinking. But, *"noli me tangere"* said Christ to His loving Mary Magdalene, she who was first to see His resurrection body. Know Me, says Christ, not according to the senses but according to the spirit: know Me interiorly, with your powers turned inward upon their object, and touch Me only with the touch of grace with which I touch you, in which is our meeting. Thus it is with our departed. Maintain and feel a sensuous remembrance of them in the flesh and you will not meet them in the unaccustomed sphere of spirit, whilst the actual strength of remembrance will diminish in time. However hard it is, however callous and cruel the course may seem, in the first weeks and months of bereavement the memory has to be refused the images which can partially supply the answer to the emptiness and cravings, and in their place is substituted the uplifting of the soul in thanksgiving. This does not mean forgetfulness, it is the preparation for that reality of communion which is going, in due course, to supersede remembrance. When you are with a person you are not in a state of remembering them, to be so would frustrate the reality of immediate relationship.

Don't let me waste your gift of death, God, by demanding what now can never be. You have given me this, chosen me for it, for your will might have been to have taken me and left him. Show me how to respond to your will. And, O God, save me. There are times when once again I am drowned in seas of misery which without warning surge over me and suck me down into their depths and down, down I have to go. That I shall never see you again, my dear, never play with you, never work, nor share all that made life real; how can we be divided? What now is the purpose of life? And further, there is this current of pain that sometimes I failed you, I refused you, I hurt you: the things that can never be undone, this is further grief, and what can I do with this weight of regret that I cannot undo or amend the thousands of sins against love? I agree that my suffering is deserved as just punishment, that it can provide some revenue for my debt. But I also learn how what was done amiss in time can be understood and swallowed up in the compassion of eternity, where God's forgiveness is a largesse upon which all can draw; I see new realities of forgiveness, its wonderful mercy. Already I have learnt this experientially, gratefully, but through my agony; that in time I shall be free of it, this is the assurance I need. When I think that the worst must be over, suddenly grief swells again to an anguish for which there seems no relief: where does it come from, that suddenly I am thrown by it? Oh, that I could let go! Is it myself, hugging itself in its own pity, wanting relief for its own sake, yearning for commiseration? The answer then is to gather up all these waves of pain and let them engulf the woe of the whole world which is suffered, endured, held up to the Father on the crucifix. This is not my particular and private grief, it is part of the sorrow of the world which is both the price and the defeat of evil. I see the great pool of suffering like spilt blood, and my work at this moment is to be part of the swab which slowly absorbs it, cleans the place, removes the stain. All suffering is one, and its final resolution and transformation is in the heart of God on calvary. As myself is worn away I shall be the more efficient instrument in the work of reparation. Suffer I must, and suffering is suffering: how should I know it unless I feel it? And it will work its own cure. This is the stupendous truth, which only experience can reveal. It will pass, it really will, this agony: from the heart of her own trouble my wise friend promised me this. And ever and again I will compel myself to answer the pain with the great swell-stop of thanksgiving to God and in God. But it all takes time, time in which I must be patient. My days seem to pass outside the normal flow of time, for three days seem three years and I am restless, unquiet, impatiently waiting, for each day seems endless and without purpose, as time stands still. "Each day dies with sleep," says the poet, but I am denied the comfort of that death; for since my Day has died my days will not sleep, emptiness is too vast for repose. O, to let go! That is the common plea of the bereaved. The only answer is the commonplace that one learns by doing and doing takes time. By disallowing the faculties their hold, detaching oneself in heart and mind gently but firmly from the images and desires which flood consciousness, in perseverance cutting the mental and emotional cords, one receives peace and interior quiet. Life will yet have a richness and a glow, there will be purpose and a restoration of meaning: not at all the same, yet certain, yet valid.

How clearly now I perceive the truth of loving people in God as a reality of experience deeper than loving God in people. This is displayed and known particularly at the altar. When we come to the communion we face beyond all feeling and sensible awareness the truth that the living and dead are united in one great reality, God who is Life. There is no need for us to think or argue, for faith becomes accepted knowledge: 'I hope, I believe, I am certain.' That the life of the Christian is in the eternities into which he is born by death is a truth enshrined in liturgy. At least since the second century, the church celebrated the Eucharist at funerals, establishing thereby communion between the living and dead in the one offering: "Look upon this oblation we humbly offer . . . that we may be profited . . . and be glorified in bliss everlasting." To offer the Eucharist on particular behalf of the faithful departed satisfies our right and proper hunger for communion with them in the only place on earth where words and spirit, things sensible and things intangible, time and eternity, are divinely appointed to meet and to co-inhere. A particular form of eucharistic worship has been developed in the church for this liturgical remembrance, whose words have especial solemnity and beauty. It is unbalanced and inadequate, to say the least of it, to spend time, energy and money on constant floral decoration of graves unless there is an equivalent fervour in attending requiems, where we are caught up in the perpetual to-and-fro movement between this world and the other where dwell our departed. Does the parish church provide this universal and traditional way of remembrance? Our churches should be packed on All Souls' Day, as we unite with all the faithful in Eucharist, all, that is, on either side of eternity's doors.

> "May my participation, O Lord, in this heavenly sacrament be for rest and life everlasting for my . . . (father and mother), and may Thy grace set its crown upon both their heads and mine."

We are in a flow of unity, and its comfort is immeasurable.

And in time, in time, there is a sun-rising, or rather, there is that gentle, almost imperceptible suffusion of light, that first flush of dawn which precedes the actual day-break. I am aware of a change, of a lightening of the pain, and of a state of assurance. An undeniable sense of pure joy sometimes fills me, and I know that this is connected with you, my dear, and that it is a joy of actual companionship, that it is fulfilment. That epigram on the old seventeenth-century tomb in lovely Burford church is only half the truth: "I go to slepe before you but we shall wake together": we are already waking together. Though absent in the body, you are yet present; but this joy comes to me, I cannot go to it: nor can I, dare I, depend upon it. But I swear to it.

> *All other ailments find in time relief.*
> *With every lapsing year my wound has bled.*

If that was the case, it was because this suffering of separation has been misused, misunderstood, repudiated as a gift. My

SEPARATION

wound will remain, yes, for one is dissevered for the rest of earthly life from a source of bliss that was a true part of one's being, but the wound is annealed beyond bleeding, it is transfigured in joy. Surely, there comes a point within the will of God when the truth is that, 'I could not love thee, dear, so much' without this very wound. God knows the point and supplies its moment.

> *Me at the dawn's first breath*
> *Thee in the dusk of death*
> *Thy love and my love tended:*
> *We shall be mother and son*
> *After all days are done*
> *All darkness ended.*

Does Newbolt sing aright? We are husband and wife, yes, mother and son, brother and sister, but in God, not in any way apart from the Eternal Light, and therefore perhaps the relationship is given only for the darkness of time. So go, beloved, go on into that Light. I would not keep you, will not desire to feel or think you. Shall we be husband and wife? That does not matter: terms of relationship are not everlasting, but love is eternal and love is life. The soul would die without love, and Jesus, it cannot die. I am content, for our love in Love is timeless. Thanks be to God.

DEATH

And to die is different from what anyone supposed, and luckier
Walt Whitman

It is in silence that we come closest to one another in human love: to walk hand-in-hand and to embrace without words is fullest speech, as all lovers know. It is in silence that we receive deep apprehensions of truth, goodness and beauty, that the mind opens and greatness is recognised, that scales fall from our eyes and spiritually we see. Our enrichments and appreciations may later be expressed in words, in shout and laughter, and exuberantly we demand action, when experience delivered in quietude explodes in energy. There are many levels or modes of silence, each with its own disclosures. Enclosed in deep silence are the moments when we know the touch of God and respond to His pressure, and as that is what He designs for us He provides the medium. One of the glories of space is its provision of silence which can be recognised quite early in life as a reality rich in blessing. "In the great spaces," said Laura Wilder with a child's insight, "in the great spaces there is an enormous stillness that makes you feel still and when you are still you can feel great stillness coming closer." It is this great silence of wide spaces which can expand the soul into dimensions beyond the senses, where it breathes the air of God.

Vast stretching expanses are sanctuaries where the still small voice of God and the answering whisper of the created spirit are antiphonal, but without their choirs such places can be empty and oppressive. It is the privilege and duty of exploring man to name the Name of God across the wide emptinesses of the world and to seal them for Him with His conquering sign. Calmly the bread and wine await the consecrating priest and just so nature quietly awaits man's ministry. Space is as the shadow of the celestial places where communication is all silent and all alive.

Though nothing in itself but an absence of sensory activity, silence asserts its positive and essential value as a vessel holding precious realities which cannot be made available to us except within its enclosing walls. How receive the wine without the chalice? Knowledge is given and truth made known in every kind of experience, there is no state, activity or occasion which is not a disclosure, but it is in rest and tranquillity that man adopts it into his functioning self, makes it vital to his personal use. The more profound and universal the truth discovered, the more embracing is the perceptive silence. Growth in the love of people, growth in the knowledge of creation, growth in the life of the spirit, all require growth in the use and love of silence; and this we either choose or refuse. Progress in life in all its modulations (to Gabriel Marcel I owe the insight of that word) is measured by the need for inward silence. Circumstances and duties may deny or limit its external safeguards and satisfactions but whatever the outward noise the spirit will seek its necessary depths of inwardness as surely as a plummet searches its levels; a crowded coach will not prevent prayer. All depends upon the soul's degree of spirituality and strength, for, as Saint Teresa said, "It is in an immense silence that the soul and God enjoy each other," a silence in which all the soul's inclinations, thrustings and images are asleep and the will is securely delivered in love to the unity of God: the silence, then, of rest.

This is what the rich young ruler (who is in all of us) turns away from, this silence which appears as the negation of great possessions; it is what the worldling refuses and what the wicked fear, for it discloses man to himself as he is in the light of God, uncovers him as he is in himself without God and without love of the neighbour. Silence reveals emptiness and its rejection spells it. The world, the flesh and the devil take refuge from Deity in cascades of noise, in torrents of words: not in true communication, which is an exchange in joy and mirth, but in idle words. Talk, talk, talk of nothing at all, look aimlessly, listen superficially, for this will hide those hollows of silence in which something may be demanded of the soul, something unpleasant revealed, some intimation be given of judgement. "The earth was still when God arose to judgement." It will be required of me eventually that 'my soul be silent unto God' for this very purpose. The Hebrews had stillness and silence in their very bones, for they were of the stock of desert nomads. All men have the place for still silence within their depths, all men need it for their whole health, but some far more than others are aware of their need and recognise that they cannot come to fruition without it. In all ages and lands there have been men impelled to live with quietude in order to live at all. In desert and wilderness, on lonely little islands, in caves, huts, houses, they have lived long lives in great peace with the single-eyed purpose of glorifying God. They did not choose the hidden ways in order to escape from anything but to advance swiftly to something, to that perfect love of God which is life eternal. Though invariably this kind of life is accompanied by massive self-denials, often of terrifying degrees, its adherents are united in their universal claim that through their choice they have found their hearts' desire, the pearl of great price, union with God: and an essential condition is silence. One of the first impressions of a visitor to a Religious house and its chapel is of the profound strength and vibrant warmth of the all-embracing silence. O precious and most lovely stillness in which the soul breathes deeply of the air of grace, hears without words the divine Word, knows without sight the presence of God, in which it is all enwrapt in love.

But it is neither possible, desirable nor deigned that all men should enter the desert of vowed monastic observance; the spiritual desert has to be made within the ordinary ways of life and within the dedicated spirit, found within the home, office, school, factory and in every vocation. When the blessed Charles de Foucauld answered his call to live a secluded life of asceticism and prayer in a Saharan oasis he built his outer-enclosure 'wall' simply of lines of small pebbles. Any child could have swept away that symbolic boundary, but to the hermit it was the token of spiritual withdrawal and it represented the reality of his rule and intention. Just so can a soul plot its invisible boundaries in which, in the midst of external activity and clamour, true silence will take root, grow and reign. Greatness has always come out of the desert and requires the desert: every devout soul will make its own quiet places, within and without.

And how richly the all-holy God gives His created occasions of silence into which we may enter if we have patience and do not hurry. Silence delicate and smooth as a pebble, found in the calm garden which is white as snow as it lies in moonlight, found in the bright dimensions under the roofless sky where the moon has blinded the stars: silence, hot and vibrant in the shadeless and empty canyon, clear and courageous in the bare aseptic hospital-ward. Even in the noise of the crowded city street there stands a church whose walls should cradle silence for the comfort of harassed humanity; but we need to know the way in. Where do we find the churches whose open doors invite and whose calm, restful interiors, designed for the praise of the Blessed Trinity, assist men to enter and use the stillness of adoration, of penitence and strength against temptation? A church can indeed be open but it may be a barren landscape of heavy pews disturbed only by the discomforts of organ-practice. Is it a place where children like to run for a quick minute of at-home-ness with God? That church ministers most faithfully to its members when it trains and sustains them in ways of prayer and recollection, in personal devotion within the solidarity of fellowship and corporate worship, without which religion is threadbare. Most faithful and true to its vocation is that part of the body of Christ which adequately provides in its liturgical worship for a proper proportion of quiet, maintaining the balance between corporate and personal expression of devotion. Far too often Anglicanism seems to hold boisterously to a belief that without hymns you cannot be saved: hymns everywhere, hymns anyhow, hymnboards of hymns, and relevancy of no account; which in effect means that we shall be spared the effort of praying, therefore the necessity of having the personal knowledge, sincerity and spiritual experience which are essential to the teacher of prayer. So the vision blurs, the people are myopic and adolescents lapse in their hundreds. Of course there is a right and welcome place for hymns, in groups, carol-parties, pilgrimages, processions, missions, when everyone's wills and emotions can be trusted to be similarly ready to be centred with much the same sentiments upon the things of God. But the singing of subjective verses of doubtful theology, mediocre standard and out-of-date terminology at moments of great solemnity is indefensible. We are not pre-fabricated identicals. "There followed a silence in heaven, about the space of half an hour": many services fail to be heavenly because they are unquiet.

More certain than anything we know about our life is that there will come a last moment when for evermore our world will be folded up in a shroud of silence. Summoned from its body, severed from all sense, each spirit's entry into life eternal must surely be within unimaginable depths of quiet; and if that silence be a milieu already loved and welcome for what it offers it will be neither strange nor alien. The speech of God's kingdom must be the same on either side of the door of death, if it is familiar to us in this world it will be welcome to us in the next: we go and come in silence.

The silent stillness of sleep, 'the counterfeit of death', is often used in simile and pictorially but though it may be called death's brother, it is a warm and rosy one with continuous breathing and it never holds full silence. "Sleep is a death, O make me try, by sleeping, what it is to die." Though the familiarity and comfort of sleep may make it an acceptable symbol of mortality, perhaps we wrong sleep and are dishonest with death if we refuse to go beyond the simile in the announcement of a decease. Death is no sleep, for sleep breathes, and how great a mystery lies in the breath of life, a mystery never really uncovered by any biological explanation of air, valves, lungs. True, our last nightly breaths can indeed be a tender and precious preparation for death when we form the habit of charging them with the Name of God. "Glory be to the Father . . . into Thy Hands I commend my spirit . . . Lord, now let me depart in peace." Each bird to its own nest, but nothing expresses our final homing better than the Nunc Dimittis, which for centuries has had its place in the last of the day's Divine Offices. The sigh which in life can reveal so much reveals also death: the last breath, it is the soul's leave-taking. Blessed is that soul whose ultimate breath is so winged with detachment and love that it lifts it light as thistledown through the doors of eternity.

So, you must look on towards your death. Why refuse and exclude the thought of that which when it comes will be the instant more supremely charged with depths of purpose than any other since your birth? It is, it already is, a moment prepared by the Father in the same creating Almightiness as was that birth, as was your rebirth by baptism into the heavenly kingdom. We receive our birth, we receive our death. It is the refusal to wait upon that receiving and the determination to take which makes suicide so proud and futile an act: yet when its cause lies in fear and weakness, even pride must surely be absolved in mercy. Our Lord said almost nothing about the beginning and end of life except to remark that the death of even an insignificant bird was within the will of God. "Your Father knows": and if a bird, how much more a son. The heavens know. So we must prepare for death with the same reverent wonder as any instructed parent prepares for a birth; not with anxiety, morbid preoccupation or narrow selfishness, but with acceptance and trust, humility and even with longing, for it is "a going to bed to take rest sweeter than slepe". There is nothing trite in the truism that we prepare for death by life. What preparation of perfection lay in Bede's end.

> "So they held him up on the pavement and he chanted,
>   Glory be to the Father and to the Son and to the Holy Ghost.
>   Then as he named the Holy Ghost his spirit took leave
>   And departed to the heavenly Kingdom."

After a life of dedication to the Glory the saintly monk arrived at its end with the simplicity and hope of perfect sacrifice. But any life may, by the mercy of God, be remade at death, for a death-bed repentance and renewal is a reality, for which God's providence may design a long bed.

For death is indeed a sacrifice both imposed upon us and offered to us, and our training in life and by the church should prepare us to enter into that state of offering. Your death has already been died by Christ whose member you are, on the bed of the cross He took it into His, you go through your death with Him and into eternal life through Him. His death was an oblation, in Him shall yours be this. In your body, in the mode of natural existence, you will be alone, and it is that condition of lonely separation, of division from all other human persons, which holds the wretchedness and darkness of death; to be met by the fortitude which is yours within the baptismal gifts of faith, hope and love. Sinful man's return to God requires this price of the severance of body and soul, this dissolution of the natural person which is the pang of death. As your spirit is potentially already in God because He is in it, your death is a return, and to the act of returning you must give yourself with all desire, all energy of will; answering death with the ready and joyful assent which, with all humility, you have always given to the silver trumpet-call of life's solemn occasions, from the font onwards."Do you?" "I do." "Will you?" "I will." There will be no further decisions, so the fullness of intention is gathered up into this finality, 'Father into thy hands': but only through the Redeemer Lord Christ, whose own mighty return was an offering made entirely on behalf of all men, an offering infinitely creative in which God eternally rejoices. Within His death which contains ours we also must offer with a definite intention, for world-peace, Christian unity, the conversion of our nation: blessings are needed everywhere and we are moving swiftly to the very Source of Blessing. Even though anyone should die suddenly, by accident, the special intention is there in the soul. From an unprepared death, God deliver us, but there is nothing to stop us from beginning our preparation today. God alone knows whether we shall have the privilege of the last sacraments, with holy anointing to cheer our last hours, but every communion and confession are potentially last and are preparations for a good death. How majestic is God in His timing of death, taking people at the one and only moment when they should be taken. The sudden death of a young and happy parent or of a fine and promising child may to the world seem cruel, unjust, wasteful, and the trail of grief, pain and problems which it brings causes great resentment and perplexity. Years may elapse before those involved in the tragedy harvest the fruits of their experience, and the rightness of the moment is revealed and the purpose justified; it becomes clear that in no other way than through death as it came would certain truths have been disclosed and accepted, insights precious and life-giving, only to be received through suffering worked out in time. God cannot err; there may, though, be a Job's life of argument before there is agreement, for some are meant to argue with Deity while others have to adore.

Why, then, this conspiracy of silence which seems to surround our contemporary western attitude to death? Perhaps it stems from the terrible, relentless bombardment of slaughter which man has given to man in this century, not so much by the violence of war as by the devilish planning of extermination, under carefully calculated conditions unthinkable for so-called civilised people. Have our perceptions been anaesthetised by the unbroken process of signing death-warrants, which has placed mortality out of all proportion to life? In earlier centuries man was not so reticent in his acknowledgement of death, he was not unwilling to uncover its features and explore its impact. Sculpture and mural paintings in and about mediaeval churches might depict an allegorical figure, usually a skeleton, accosting people and leading them away to its hall of death: three kings out hunting, full of life, are thus dramatically faced with their end. The famous engravings of Holbein which display the Dance of Death illustrate its interest for the imagination in the late Middle Ages. Epitaphs give eloquent reminders of the coming end, sculptured skeletons lie on cathedral tombs, skulls are cut on stones and have an accepted place in paintings, not as macabre objects but as emblems of mankind's universal experience. There can be no more tender and reverent reminder of death than El Greco's picture of Saint Francis displaying a skull to a young and fervent friar. All these representations are not signs of an unbalanced melancholia or of an exaggerated concern with morbid phantasies, they simply show what is immensely relevant to serious life, they assume that death is accepted as 'the privilege of human nature'.

"I die daily," said Saint Paul, and symbolically this is a just claim, for none of the apostles endured a greater variety of 'deaths', the tale of which he does not hesitate to recount when he presents his credentials for authority; and in his ardour for 'life in the Kingdom of the Son of His love' he dies in his continuous daily struggle with his own 'old man', that sin-riddled self which he renounced in baptism. Paul indeed has been so successful in his warfare against himself that he can claim that "the life I now live is not mine but the life which Christ lives in me." No longer is it Paul in action, for he is dead to himself; it is Christ: yet every second of the day it is really the live Paul who is making way for Christ. Spiritual writers have always described this discipline of ceaseless self-denial, technically called asceticism or mortification, as a process of dying through which alone comes freedom to live in Christ. In our day the insight of that spiritual giant amongst men, Teilhard de Chardin, has given us a new word for these metaphorical deaths, which are both served to us by our circumstances and taken upon us in our strivings after perfection: he speaks of them as diminishments. That which Saint Paul calls the old Adam, the old man, our imperfect nature with its disposition to sin, is remade into whole and perfect nature through its successive purifying diminishments, the last of which is the extinction of life in this world, the real and actual death. If we could rather carefully keep that word for this one tremendous and inevitable climax of diminishment perhaps we as Christians could present to the world a clearer and less maimed, less hesitant acceptance of death, a conception which would both safeguard its solemnity and be fearless of conventionality.

For there surely can be no more solemn moment than that designed for the return of a man's spirit, naked in its essence, to his Creator, for the surrender of the son to the majesty and wonder of the divine Father; and the stillness and silence which inevitably envelops the empty body should be respected. The hall of death is compacted of silence. The laying-out of the dead is a vicarious service of reticence and withdrawal, a modesty, and it is an affront to man's dignity, a travesty of his true nature, to embellish and glorify a lifeless corpse as if it were something in itself, to make a spectacle of what is an emptiness in which decay is already at work; that the holy death of a holy person leaves a corpse which is a picture serene, regal, joyful, beautiful, does not at all alter the sense of its emptiness and the absence of all presence. A public lying-in-state is a different matter, for it is an occasion for paying tribute and honour to a great and grand man, as the strewing of flowers and the burning of lights around the departed is witness of our last loving admirations and gratitudes. All this witnesses to the reality of our belief in the communion of saints, and the desire to touch the catafalque of some great one departed whose life showed massive holiness is itself an act of prayer proclaiming faith in eternal life. Although of course there is grief, just and valid, at our loss of someone who would seem to be so vital to our own and the general need, yet as we attend the last rites we should share a sense of triumph with and for them, for whom 'all the trumpets sound on the other side', and we should most certainly feel full gratitude for their true home-going.

How mysterious is the impress that the character of the dead can impose on a funeral, which may be anything from a sad, superficial and dispiriting affair, from which we are relieved to hurry, to a strong joyful act of thanksgiving and praise, a grand affirmation of mercy and hope which lifts all present closer to the heavenlies, so that for a few short but exalted moments the doors of eternity seem almost to open and disclose the light into which the departed has entered. With Boethius we do indeed "Look to the highest heights of heaven", and we see more than "the stars in their ancient peace". Sadness for the parting but also, and far more enduring, thankful joy for the consummation, are the two threads in the shuttle which weaves the fabric of a Christian funeral. Too often we have to endure travesties of truth in the ghastly hymns which thoughtless ecclesiasticism allows to remain in the books and be used; if, for instance, death means that we are simply going to fall into a state of 'sleeping, sleeping, sleeping' it hardly seems worth the trouble of dying; we might as well be extinct. Is God a dream? No dogma of Christian belief is plainer than that death translates us into life in Christ who is God all-holy, altogether lovely, the centre and source of being. What has come over us Christians that we should squint sideways at death, disguising our references to it by oblique phrasing? Our belief and hope should be sound enough to counteract society's all too frequent and all-worldly efforts to hide from the mortally sick the imminence of death, so denying them their rightful opportunity to prepare to meet the Bridegroom. On the contrary, we should help to fill their lamps with the oil of preparation. 'Oh no, I don't want the Vicar to call, she might think she was dying.' That is not the attitude of the children of our Father. We need to be at home with the reality of death, to grow towards it in trust and hope; for because it has its sure and certain place in life it should be welcome, since together they form one complete design. Death, welcome: but in God's time and because it is His will.

Never, though, should familiarity with death mean a facile and superficial approach which ignores its mystery, for a mystery holds awe. We dare not minimise death, which has its valley of shadows; it is quite normal that at some time or other a man should experience a fear and dread of it. It is an impending event uniquely unknown to each individual consciousness and it is suffered alone, and in prospect the very strangeness defying pre-knowledge may well be terrifying. Once more we are faced with polarity, and the tension may be costly, but rewarding when we handle it. We pray that as regards death we may be neither glib nor fearful, and we know that we shall be given grace to endure to the end: that is the heavenly promise. On the one hand, the psalmist with lovely faith declares that even in the unknown valley he will fear no evil for the Lord is with him; on the other, that same Lord Himself warns us that the prince of evil is the one thing we should fear for it has the power to destroy us. The snake of evil with its stench and its horror will attack everyone in its hope of finding a place for itself, and Christ Himself was prepared for its attack, though He said it would find no place in Him. We are ignorant of how and when the prince of this world will attempt to establish a trading-post in the city of the soul, and although our besetting sins should be warnings of approach, we often fail to recognise the first insinuations of the evil one. "I can't think why I said that, I don't really think so," is a friend's explanation of some alien element which suddenly startled us in an unexpected expression. From childhood onwards we have had our temptations and conflicts, our particular fears, darknesses, sometimes inexplicable but swamping sorrow, varying in intensity and duration from one individual to another even as the grain varies with the wood. O to save our children from these seas of pain! But this we cannot do, in fact we may sometimes be their cause. Each one has to meet his own woe, but its weight will never be greater than he can bear, and invariably there comes release. And all these disturbances of peace and security, these separations from felicity, are preparations for the separation of death; they help to shape us to our final end. The agonies which sometimes a soul endures on account of sin and the poverty of its repentances, its pains when God deprives it of the light and bliss of His presence which is its very life, its depths of sorrow when it is flooded by endless interior desolations and exterior unhappinesses, more than anything else serve to loosen it from its very self and to lighten that fettering burden, which can the more easily be cast off when the call comes to wade the waters of death. The sorrow of death, of which Jesus spoke, it may be suffered some time before the end, indeed be a warning, this cloud of deep depression and gloom which descends upon the soul, obscuring its interior senses so that all things fair and sweet are darkened and God Himself seems absent. "Why hast Thou forsaken me?" But the wedding-garment of grace has been donned, no one can remove it, and however black the darkness and intense the conflict with its ruler, my God is there, and the wood of the saving cross upholds. Always light breaks through before the end and there is glory. But it is our duty to pray often and regularly for the dying.

Of Christ's death, the writer to the Hebrews says that it was an entering into the holy place. There is great richness in this concept of entering: in fact, all the days of our life can be seen as a succession of entries into life; and of course there can be refusals. It is because in that last moment of unutterable quietude the faithful servant is going home to the place prepared for him by Christ, that we cannot think of death as a passive reception of dissolution but as our energy of entering into newness of life. Already awaiting us is a state, a mode of being, the mode of the redeemed which was perceived even by the people of the Old Testament. So it is not with a passive resigned mind, which is often the poet's attitude to death, but with longing eagerness to be worthy of God's summons that a Christian desires, with Saint Paul, "to depart and be with Christ". Is my soul athirst for the living God? If in life then also in death.

Yet no Christian may ever lose sight of the purity and holiness of the living God, nor avoid His judgement. Emily Brontë may declare, splendidly and triumphantly:

> *There is no room for Death*
> *Nor atom that his might can render void;*
> *Thou, Thou are Being and Breath,*
> *And what Thou are can never be destroyed.*

and upon that hangs a pantheistic conclusion. Her poem reveals no insight into the blinding ineffable purity of the Thou before whom spotless angels veil their faces. The Godhead is in light unapproachable and whatever the hymn to Mithras may say, it is not only that light which hides Him from us but it is our sinhood. Before we can be lost in wonder, love and praise as we sing the full song of the redeemed, we sinners have to bear the unimaginable pain of confrontation with God's burning absolute goodness, of seeing ourselves against it. The experience has never been more sensitively described than by John Henry Newman in his great poem *The Dream of Gerontius*, in which spiritual clarity is matched by immaculate expression. We cannot doubt but that, after the vision, we too shall cry to be removed to the lowest deeps where, loathing our sinhood, we shall be purified, made whole and complete and thus able to bear the eternal Beauty. The sharpest pain of purification must be that the sword is double-edged, dealing twin wounds of unfulfilled longing to dwell forever with the celestial glory of God's Face and freezing emptiness of unworthiness ever to come before it. So with all our strength and perseverance we give ourselves now, in time, to the chosen work of penitence as an essential condition of our entering into death: then, the cleansing power already at work interiorly, we know that however great the sin it will, through the Redeemer Christ's love, be judged by the Mercy, to whom we dare to fly on wings of faith and contrition. So long as we remain in the body we cannot be rid of a sense of sin, which will fluctuate in its intensity: but it is of sin forgiven; this is perpetually enlarging our joyful trust in our Saviour whose Name above all names spells mercy, truth and peace. This trust it is which can spring us clear-eyed to death, which we meet with Jesus on our lips,

Jesus joy of all hearts, whose joy cannot be taken from us. Death, the moment of attained joy.

There are two instinctive and universal modes of expressing joy common to all creation, namely, movement and sound. In man these become dance and music, increasing in complexity as he develops. For ancient and for primitive peoples dancing is integral to the seasonal routines of life and is customary at all its most significant occasions, such as marriage, death, war, victory and so on; it is an accepted social expression, sometimes it is a regular part of religious rites, and may even produce and reveal mystical exaltation. As dancing involves the entire body and demands concentrated sensuous activity, it was recognised that, though it could express religious emotions, it was easily debased and could provoke dangerous excesses of sensuality leading perhaps to moral degradation: so it was relegated by highly civilised peoples to the lower orders, and to professional dancers, whose entertainments could provide enjoyment. At times dancing has met with active opposition from religious authorities because of its worldly character and possible degrading influence. Music, on the contrary, involves the body hardly at all (*pace* some eminent conductors!), it requires a minimum of physical movement and sensory activity but it demands the response and concentration of mental faculties. Music inheres primarily in rhythm, that is, in the breaking of sound and a development of beat. Is the influence and satisfaction of rhythm due to its ability to carry a person's consciousness forward and beyond the state of psychical inactivity, immobility and coldness? For it is essentially a flow and a pulse of an ongoing process, it is progressive, and as it is integral to growth to move forward, onward in progression, it is not fanciful to see the principle of rhythm as ontological in creation. Indeed it may be because of this ontological necessity that personality is healthy and satisfied when a man's faculties senses and muscles are employed in a well-ordered rhythm of activity and rest, work and recreation. But unbroken rhythm ends in dull automation, and it is as well to remember that there is an endless variety of rhythms and that one can be imposed on another, which is immensely stimulating and exciting. And rhythm, which is the regularity of simple beat, cannot for long continue unaccompanied by variation in stress, when the sound will swell and diminish, elongate and shrink, as it does in speech: thus comes melody. Any small child at play can demonstrate that even two notes may, with rhythm, become the foundation of simple if monotonous chanting.

Although dance and music are interdependent, fundamentally united by rhythm and contributing richly the one to the other, music is immeasurably the superior in its possession of the quality of intangibility; its existence is unrelated to bodily and representational images, it can be independent of ideas. Though it contributes value and enhancement to imaginations and emotions, even to ideas, though they may need music for their expression, it in its heights exists without them; it is something essentially itself, indescribably unclothed except with itself. 'The swift and nimble wings of music' can lift a man out of himself, carry him into exalted regions of the spirit which satisfy his noblest longings and confirm deep intimations of realities, mysteriously nourishing his whole being. Granted that this assumes music in its purest, most refined and sublime forms (which is by no means synonymous with technically religious music), but that is a fair assumption, for true understanding of anything whatsoever is obtained only by a knowledge of that thing in its perfection.

Amongst all men's pursuits and arts, the immateriality of

music is unique: not dissimilar from mathematics, it is comparable to the soul's acts of virtue and to pure contemplation. Can music fail, then, to carry the imprint of eternal value? It uncovers the soul, enlarges, uplifts and moves within it by hidden, unseen means; herein it is like the prayer of contemplation, which is without words, without images, empty of sense and emotion, filling the soul with naked bliss. Contemplation is an is-ness and so ultimately is music; the difference between them lies in the nature of the is-ness of the prayer, which is essentially loving rest in the presence of its sublime and personal Object of adoration. But music can express and do for the soul what prayer does, that is, provide it with a medium of joy, fulfilment, of wonder and worship: the ultimate end of all beauty. And for the right listener this can be said of any music anywhere, if its intention is pure: Sir Thomas Browne may be rare but he is not singular in finding that 'vulgar and tavern music does not make him either mad or merry' but arouses his deep devotion as he thinks upon the first Composer.

The first Composer. That music is directly and immediately derived from the Creator of the universe was an idea conceived by man in the early ages of western philosophy and accepted as an unquestioned concept for over two thousand years. The origin of this belief lies in the science of number and in astronomy as directed by Pythagoras. His calculations of the heavenly bodies and their order, their controlled motions and 'silent march, obedient as an army' through space, positive and unfailing as truth, generated the notion of their harmony; hence the theory of the music of the spheres. Though this might not be perceptible to human ears it was demonstratively available to man's intellect. And behind the starry bodies revolving in their courses, endlessly producing the harmony that is the result of their mathematical relationship, is their Mighty

DEATH

and eternal Creator whose majestic design is itself the source of their music. Thus the Pythagorean theories explained the celestial origin of music which man receives from the heavens, enters into, and makes part of his inheritance. This was among the accepted world-ideas common to all men of Shakespeare's day and not disdained by Milton, for his readers must have been sufficiently familiar with it to accept his representation of the Creator setting the constellations in their places to the sound of the first-begotten song of these His sons of the morning. Does any English poem declare the perfection of 'music sphere-descended' more gloriously than Milton's *Hymn on the Morning of Christ's Nativity*?

But by his day the time was at hand, had in fact already begun, when man, ever developing and evolving, began to see himself as sole creator of the beauty and wisdom of art and science, as containing within himself by his own right and sufficiency the pulsing blood of conception and creation. When in the brilliant light of the Renaissance he began to accept and worship himself as the reason and centre of life, his sense of depending upon and entering into celestial glories, which though present and evaluated in time are created in eternity, inevitably diminished, receded, even vanished.

To depend means initially to hang from, to hang upon, to cling to. "So hangs my soul upon God," sang the psalmist and that word in the Hebrew original means to cling and cleave to. The image of humanity hanging upon an invisible Source and owning dependence, seemed to aspiring man to insult his natural greatness, and to suggest a lack of virility. It was an abdication of personal responsibility, a servile diminishment of his will. But to hang upon, to cleave to, the breasts of the Eternal means neither inertia nor supine helplessness nor servitude, all of which are a contradiction of the energy demanded from the man who chooses the way of obedience and love, whose purpose is perfection. Watch the tiny bird clinging to the net of fat suspended from the branch of the apple-tree, notice its astonishing energy and activity as it attacks its nourishment and you will see what *'pendere'* means, and approve the use of the word 'depend'. In abandoning his sense of dependence upon God man deprived himself of both the impulse to adore and the need to pray; for prayer is the soul's art of entering into relationship with Deity, a relationship which, we must continually remind ourselves, is divinely and timelessly prevenient and present. As man through his self-elevation and extension loses his acknowledged need and inner experience of the transcendent and eternal God he becomes increasingly enmeshed in the web of passing time and in the immanence of being: which leads to despair, to ignorance, to darkness: like a falling star.

Has this seemed a meandering and aimless discursion, cheating us of our purpose and place as if we are ourselves fallen stars? Indeed it has not led us from our course, we have but revolved on our axis and we are back at the beginning, enlarged by vast vistas. Music, with its origin within the will of God, abides as the expression of pure joy: death is the silent act which springs man into swift unresisting movement towards the sole Source of all Joy, joy in measure beyond our measuring: that movement, then, is the moment of celestial harmony transcending sound. With death the unimaginable becomes real in the marriage of silence and music.

GLORY

"All authority, all power, is given to Me in heaven and upon earth" are the last words of Jesus reported by Matthew. About to leave the one for the other, the Resurrected Lord deliberately joins them together, the earthly and the unearthly, in one domain which is dominatd by His ἐξουσία; and where there is ἐξουσία there is δόξα. In His power shines His glory, His glory pronounces power. Gazing at his disappearing figure the apostles responded with worship and so began their heavens, for that moment most filled with worship is most full of heaven. This is the strength of the martyrs; they worship and adore even in torment unto death, so there is glory and the power given to continue in martyrdom: their heaven begins. No wonder that the young church breakfasted on glory, as Charles Williams typically said.

Heaven. There is nothing to say beyond what has been said in the moral and spiritual vision of John's Apocalypse and spread before our stunned gaze by the inspired, mighty genius of Dante. Other men are Miltons without the sublime insights and power to go beyond Paradise Lost. Why should they? For the Lord Himself said little about the place He had come from, which He called heaven, essentially the place of our Father. Like prayer, He took it for granted. His omission has its purpose. He knows that we are too space-minded to be able to think about a place which is no place according to natural dimensions, so He would have us consider God, whom it is our true happiness to know, love and serve. Indeed, heaven can mean nothing to us unless we have a yearning for God; and the more the soul is possessed by yearning the less is it concerned to speculate about His place: though such a possession is a gift bestowed only by grace on the ardent servant and son of the Blessed Trinity. The cleverness of this age tries to refuse place, to ignore the tangible and refuse nature in favour of the dilatation of the mind. But no one in this world can live on abstraction except in so far as he approaches the 'pure light intellectual full-charged with love', which is an unsurpassable definition given by Dante of heaven. Yet Jesus speaking as a man gives heaven, where He is preparing our place, dimension.

We cannot guess at heaven, but we watch its King for any hints He may drop. Such is His greeting when He comes suddenly upon all His apostles, undisguised and recognisably Himself in His resurrection body. "Peace to you," He says. Peace. He has not led them to expect it. Not peace but a sword had been His promise, with rifts and antagonisms in their families, and persecutions. He had enjoined peace-making as a condition for happiness, but that was a matter for active promotion, not an entry into a passive state. All through Christ's teaching runs the note of doing, asking, seeking; an urgency of growth is to be the lot of His disciples, no static state of achievement. The peace which He gives them is, then, of celestial origin and it is an interpenetration of earth by heaven. We may in fact judge how much of heaven we know and acknowledge by the peace of our hearts, whatever external tumult and strife surrounds us. Peace depends upon the reconciliation of opposites, the harmony of contraries, and the greater the opposition the greater strength of divine life is required for the triumphant attainment of unity.

This opens a further window on eternity. Peace is not a peace of one but of many. These chapters which have explored the journey of the soul along this life's inevitable ways of suffering and their claims upon it for obedience, submission, sacrifice and so on, have been concerned with the individual. There has been little enough about corporate life and shared society with its richness and responsibilities, there has been an absence of accent on the group, whereas people of today are apt to be expressively group-conscious, finding inspiration and strength in collective thinking and activity. But the Lord's greeting of 'peace' is a reminder that heaven has no solitudes though it has all the blessing which in this life we, as did Jesus, realise only in individual solitude. For us, as for Him, retreats are a necessity, and days depend upon nights. The peace of heaven contains and is contained by society, it is a union and unity of persons, a kingdom thronged with all who live in, by and through love. Always we find ourselves being brought back to love, and if it is ultimate Love there is nothing further to be said, for there is God, there is glory.

> *O Light eternal, who only in thyself abidest,*
> *alone thyself dost understand, and to thyself,*
> *self-understood and understanding, turnest*
> *love and smiling.*

Dante, of course, but as someone said, you cannot live on Dante, even though you can't live without him. Is it fair to end in heaven when we live on earth? Especially as we have to acknowledge that in those places and at those moments when heaven is most tangibly at our disposal and we most desire to adore we are more than likely to have, as we say, no feelings. It is common to us all to be least aware of God, least devout and quick in offering that worship and homage we long to present, at the time of prayer and sacrament, even at the Eucharist when we acknowledge His actual presence. Week after week, perhaps day after day, the faithful communicant, the faithful priest, comes to the altar, and not even there the holy words, the mighty action, the miracle of presence, can prevent inattention, emptiness of mind and heart, even motions of distaste and irritation. He struggles to concentrate, to be devout, to offer a heart of love and a strength of intercession within the Lord's offering, but the will is like a bucking horse, and feelings can never be commanded. He is dispirited and ashamed that he is so much of the earth, earthy at the heavenly table, which he knows he really loves; yet all he can do is to ignore the weaknesses and trivialities which accompany human nature, persevere in the bounden duty and service and, having done all, to stand. That is enough, all that is asked, to stand: not to feel. Then one day, at the heavenly time of the Lord's coming he may, with the unexpectedness of a shooting star, be caught up in the Lord's glory, his being flooded with love for God and the beatitude of His beauty; and he will know. Faithfulness alone is crowned. It may not be Saint Paul's third heaven, but it is a heaven, a participation in divinity, an adoration of the Glory, and, supreme gift, it is impossible not to love. By this one awareness, of whatever degree and kind, the soul is strengthened for all the long days of dull dryness and inabilities which may be its lot and often its shame, those ways of growth and maturity which are so safe. But the light has shone.

We have no business and no need to expect anything out of the ordinary, for we are ordinary people. The wonder and delight is, that in all the ordinariness of life we are constantly meeting penetrations of wisdom, in the commonplace we find veins of beauty, and nowhere is there a limit to revelation.

'I am grateful for so many things'
Said the old lady who had lost everything,
'The warmth of the sun, the little flowers
Make me so happy; and I like my small chats
With the other old ladies in the home.
I can see the sea from my window
And I am doing a dear little piece of tapestry.
God has been so good to me and I glory each day
In the wonders of His creation.'

'Aw, nuts,' said the young man who had everything
holding the sun, the sea and the flowers in his hands.
'The world is a lousy place and sick to the heart.
Glory?' he said, 'wonder?' he asked. 'Goodnight.'

But of course she was right.*

Glory: and upon me, Jesus, Thy mercy.

* *Virginia Graham.*